BUSINESS ISSUES, COMPETITION AND ENTREPRENEURSHIP

CORPORATE PROFIT SHIFTING

AN EXAMINATION OF DATA, ISSUES, AND CURBS

Business Issues, Competition and Entrepreneurship

Additional books in this series can be found on Nova's website under the Series tab.

Additional e-books in this series can be found on Nova's website under the e-book tab.

BUSINESS ISSUES, COMPETITION AND ENTREPRENEURSHIP

CORPORATE PROFIT SHIFTING

AN EXAMINATION OF DATA, ISSUES, AND CURBS

DORIAN L. PETERS
EDITOR

nova publishers
New York

Library of Congress Cataloging-in-Publication Data

ISBN: 978-1-63483-767-5

Published by Nova Science Publishers, Inc. † New York

CONTENTS

PREFACE

Congress and the Obama Administration have expressed interest in addressing multinational corporations' ability to shift profits into low- and no-tax countries with little corresponding change in business operations. Several factors appear to be driving this interest. Economists have estimated that profit shifting results in significant tax revenue losses annually, implying that reducing the practice could help address deficit and debt concerns. Profit shifting and base erosion are also believed to distort the allocation of capital as investment decisions are overly influenced by taxes. Fairness concerns have also been raised. If multinational corporations can avoid or reduce their taxes, other taxpayers (including domestically focused businesses and individuals) may perceive the tax system as unfair. At the same time, policymakers are also concerned that American corporations could be unintentionally harmed if careful consideration is not given to the proper way to reduce profit shifting. This book is intended to assist Congress as it considers what, if any, action to curb profit shifting. This book discusses the methods used for shifting profits only to the extent that it is necessary for interpreting the data or discussing policy options. In addition, this book addresses tax havens; basic concepts and policy issues of U.S. international corporate taxation; and reforms of U.S. international taxation

In: Corporate Profit Shifting
Editor: Dorian L. Peters

ISBN: 978-1-63483-767-5

Chapter 1

CORPORATE TAX BASE EROSION AND PROFIT SHIFTING (BEPS): AN EXAMINATION OF THE DATA*

Mark P. Keightley and Jeffrey M. Stupak

SUMMARY

Congress and the Obama Administration have expressed interest in addressing multinational corporations' ability to shift profits into low- and no-tax countries with little corresponding change in business operations. Several factors appear to be driving this interest. Economists have estimated that profit shifting results in significant tax revenue losses annually, implying that reducing the practice could help address deficit and debt concerns. Profit shifting and base erosion are also believed to distort the allocation of capital as investment decisions are overly influenced by taxes. Fairness concerns have also been raised. If multinational corporations can avoid or reduce their taxes, other taxpayers (including domestically focused businesses and individuals) may perceive the tax system as unfair. At the same time, policymakers are also concerned that American corporations could be unintentionally harmed if careful consideration is not given to the proper way to reduce profit shifting.

* This is an edited, reformatted and augmented version of a Congressional Research Service publication R44013, prepared for Members and Committees of Congress, dated April 30, 2015.

Consistent with the findings of existing research, the analysis presented in this report provides indications that the magnitude of profit shifting may be significant. For example, of the $1.2 trillion in overseas profits American companies reported earning in 2012, $600 billion was attributed to seven tax havens: Bermuda, Ireland, Luxembourg, the Netherlands, Singapore, Switzerland, and the U.K. Caribbean Islands. The Netherlands was the most popular location to report profits, accounting for 14.1% of all overseas earnings of American companies. Further analysis reveals that the share of profits reported is significantly disproportional to the amount of hiring and investment made by American companies in these countries.

Data on the foreign direct investment (FDI) positions of American companies are also analyzed. Examining FDI data allows for an indirect investigation into the degree of profit shifting. The FDI data show that the same seven tax haven countries accounted for nearly half (47%) of the worldwide FDI position of the United States. The data also show that an increasing share of FDI is being held via holding companies. The report discusses that some of the increased use of holding companies may be tax motivated. Lastly, data from the International Monetary Fund (IMF) and the United Nations (UN) on the location of the FDI positions of all countries indicate that profit shifting is likely an international issue.

Several policy options for addressing base erosion and profit shifting are briefly discussed. Included in the discussion are the tradeoffs and considerations involved in moving closer to either a pure worldwide tax system or a pure territorial tax system. The adoption of a minimum tax or a formula apportionment system is also discussed, as well as the effects of modifying current tax policy such as broadening the definition of Subpart F income or reducing corporate tax rates. The report concludes with a discussion of the Organisation for Economic Co-operation and Development (OECD) Base Erosion and Profit Shifting (BEPS) plan, which may have implications for American corporations even if the U.S. does not adopt the OECD's recommendations.

INTRODUCTION

It has been reported with increasing frequency that American corporations are engaging in profit shifting. That is, they are using tax planning strategies to avoid, delay, or reduce their U.S. tax on income earned overseas. Included among the companies that have been mentioned are Amazon, Apple, Caterpillar, Cisco, Google, Pfizer, and Starbucks, along with a number of other well and not-so-well known businesses.[1] To curb profit shifting, some have argued for disallowing the sophisticated techniques companies use, as either part of a broader tax reform plan, or as separate legislation; presumably the separate legislation would be a stop-gap measure put in place until potential tax reform takes place. Others have argued that it is the current U.S. corporate tax rate and general approach to taxing American multinational corporations (MNCs) that is encouraging companies to shift profits and keep money abroad. The best remedy, it is argued, is to reduce the corporate rate and consider excluding most foreign earned income from taxation. This approach has also been offered as a broader tax reform package. Thus far, there is no consensus on the best way to reduce profit shifting.

Profit shifting is not exclusively a U.S. problem. Foreign policymakers have also voiced concern over the tax strategies employed by U.S. corporations operating in their markets, as well as their own domestically based corporations. For example, in 2012, the Public Accounts Committee of the British House of Commons called upon executives from Amazon, Google, and Starbucks to explain their companies' U.K. tax strategies.[2] German Chancellor Angela Merkel urged action to curb corporate profit shifting in a speech at the Organisation for Economic Co-operation and Development (OECD) on February 19, 2014.[3] Similarly, French President François Hollande has called for some form of global tax harmonization.[4]

In response to the growing international concern, the OECD was asked by the G20 finance ministers to develop an Action Plan on Base Erosion and Profit Shifting (BEPS).[5] The goal is to develop 15 detailed actions governments can take to reduce tax avoidance by multinational corporations (as well as individuals) worldwide. The Action Plan is scheduled to be completed in three phases: September 2014, September 2015, and December 2015. Some of the actions will require coordination and information sharing between governments, and potentially the amendment of existing tax treaties. As a result, the Action Plan relies heavily on the participation of all major economies. A number of G20 countries that are not part of the OECD (Argentina, Brazil, China, India, Indonesia, Russia, Saudi Arabia, and South Africa) participated in the meetings that led to the eventual adoption of the Action Plan by all G20 finance ministers.

This report is intended to assist Congress as it considers what, if any, action to curb profit shifting. Data on the operation of U.S. and foreign corporations are analyzed to understand where profit may be being shifted to and to what extent. There are indications that profits are being shifted to "tax-preferred" or "tax-haven" countries, and that the amount of profits involved (and therefore the tax revenue lost) could be considerable.[6] This report discusses the methods used for shifting profits only to the extent that it is necessary for interpreting the data or discussing policy options.

OVERVIEW OF THE U.S. INTERNATIONAL CORPORATE TAX SYSTEM

The United States, in theory, taxes American corporations on their worldwide income.[7] This approach to taxation is referred to as a worldwide (or resident-based) tax system. In contrast, a territorial (or source-based) system would tax American corporations only on income earned within the physical borders of the United States. In reality, no major economy has a pure worldwide or a pure territorial tax system.[8]

Although the U.S. taxes the worldwide income of American corporations, current law allows taxes to be deferred on income earned abroad until that income is repatriated (returned) to the United States.[9] Deferral is a benefit to American corporations because delayed taxes are a reduced tax expense to firms due to the time value of money.[10] In the extreme, deferral could allow an American corporation to completely avoid U.S. taxation on foreign source income if they never repatriate their overseas income, either because the income is being held abroad in financial assets or because it is permanently reinvested (e.g., in plant and equipment). The income earned by foreign branches of American corporations, however, cannot be deferred.[11]

A particular type of income which does not qualify for deferral is known as "subpart F income." Named for the location in the Internal Revenue Code (IRC) where its tax treatment is defined, subpart F income generally includes passive types of income such as interest, dividends, annuities, rents, and royalties.[12] The highly fungible nature of subpart F income is such that corporations can use overseas subsidiaries to transfer taxable income from high-tax countries to low-tax countries with the ultimate goal of reducing their U.S. income tax liability. To prevent this, corporations must pay taxes on subpart F income in the year it is generated, regardless of whether it is actually repatriated to the United States.[13]

A temporary exception to the subpart F income tax rules for "active financing income" existed for income earned between 1997 and 2014. The active financing exception relates to the income earned by American corporations that operate banking, financing, and insurance lines of business abroad. Although some of the income derived from these lines of business (e.g., interest, dividends, and annuities) could be labeled as passive, active financing income was excepted from subpart F, and thus qualified for deferral and was only taxed when it was repatriated to the United States. The exception was last extended retroactively through 2014 by P.L. 113-295 in the 113th Congress, and has regularly been extended in recent years as part of "tax extenders" legislation.

When American corporations repatriate income from subsidiaries operating abroad, that income may have already been taxed by a foreign country. If it has, corporations are generally allowed to claim a dollar-for-dollar tax credit (up to a limit) for foreign taxes paid. The credit, formally known as the foreign tax credit, is intended to alleviate the double taxation of corporate income.[14] The credit is generally limited to the amount of taxes a corporation would pay in the credit's absence, which is effectively just the U.S. corporate tax rate multiplied by the amount of income earned abroad. In other words, an American corporation may claim the foreign tax credit up to the point that reduces its U.S. tax on foreign-earned income to zero, but no further. Additionally, a separate credit must be calculated for two types of income "baskets"—passive and non-passive income.

As long as the U.S. corporate tax rate is higher than the foreign country's rate, the foreign tax credit should—in principle—result in the corporation owing the same amount in total taxes (U.S. plus foreign) as it would if it earned the income in the Unites States. When the foreign tax rate is higher than the U.S. tax rate, a corporation should end up paying total world taxes (U.S. plus foreign) at a tax rate higher than the U.S. rate. There are instances when a corporation could end up with "excess" foreign credits because of the limits that restrict the credit from reducing U.S. taxes owed below zero. Excess foreign tax credits generated in a high-tax country can potentially be used to reduce U.S. tax owed on income generated in a low-tax country via a process known as "cross crediting." This is possible because deferral allows corporations to selectively decide when to repatriate income and therefore when to use excess credits.

Indications of Profit Shifting by American MNCs

The tax returns of American corporations are private, which makes it difficult to study profit shifting directly. Several publically available datasets, however, do allow for an indirect examination into the extent that profit shifting may be occurring. The U.S. Bureau of Economic Analysis (BEA) collects data on the financial operations of American MNCs, including information on where they report profits, employ workers, make investments, conduct research and development, and carry out various other activities. The BEA also collects country-level data on the foreign direct investment (FDI) positions of U.S firms. The following sections discuss these data in turn.

BEA Corporate Profits by Country

American companies reported earning profits of just over $1.2 trillion abroad in 2012 according to the BEA. *Table 1* shows that the 10 most popular places to report profits were responsible for approximately 65% (or $789 billion) of the total $1.2 trillion in overseas earnings. Seven of the 10 reporting jurisdictions are considered "tax havens" or "tax-preferred" countries, including the four most popular destinations: the Netherlands, Ireland, Luxembourg, and Bermuda. The other three tax-preferred countries are Switzerland, Singapore, and the U.K. Caribbean Islands.[15] Among the non-tax-preferred countries, the United Kingdom and Canada are major industrialized nations that are historically close trading partners with the United States. Norway is the biggest oil producer in Europe and the third largest exporter of natural gas in the world, which explains its placement on the list.[16]

Table 1. Ten Most Popular Places to Report Profits for U.S. Companies, 2012

Rank	Country	Profits (millions)	Profits as % of Total Overseas Profits
1	Netherlands	$172,250	14.1%
2	Ireland	$122,328	10.0%
3	Luxembourg	$96,079	7.9%
4	Bermuda	$79,706	6.5%
5	United Kingdom	$74,141	6.1%
6	Canada	$70,782	5.8%
7	Switzerland	$57,930	4.7%
8	Singapore	$42,395	3.5%
9	UK Caribbean Islands	$40,881	3.4%
10	Norway	$32,961	2.7%
Top 10		$789,453	64.7%

Rank	Country	Profits (millions)	Profits as % of Total Overseas Profits
All Foreign Countries		$1,219,956	100.0%

Source: CRS analysis of U.S. Bureau of Economic Analysis, Outward Activities of Multinational Enterprises: Operations of U.S. Parent Companies and Their Foreign Affiliates, Preliminary 2012 Statistics.

Notes: Profits are measured as net income plus foreign taxes paid. The United Kingdom Caribbean Islands group is comprised of Cayman Islands, the British Virgin Islands, Turks and Caicos Islands, and Montserrat. The BEA does not break out data for the individual United Kingdom Caribbean Island countries.

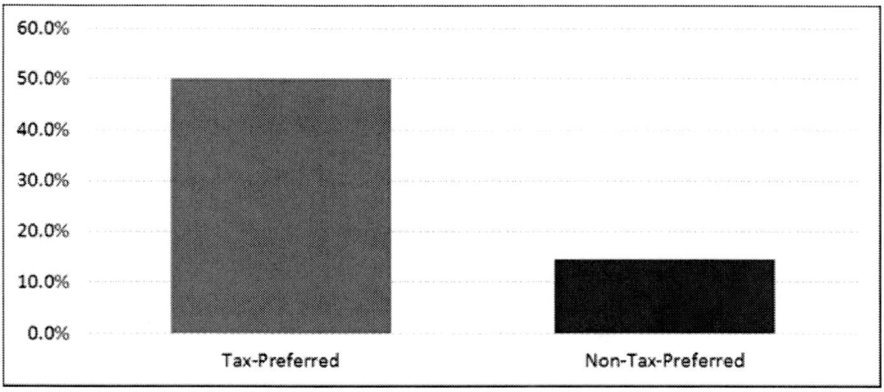

Source: CRS analysis of U.S. Bureau of Economic Analysis, Outward Activities of Multinational Enterprises: Operations of U.S. Parent Companies and Their Foreign Affiliates, Preliminary 2012 Statistics.

Notes: Profits are measured as net income plus foreign taxes paid. The tax-preferred group includes Bermuda, Ireland, Luxembourg, Netherlands, Singapore, Switzerland, and the U.K. Caribbean Islands. The non-taxpreferred group includes Canada, Norway, and the United Kingdom.

Figure 1. Share of Foreign Earned U.S. Corporate Profits in Top-10 Jurisdictions (2012).

Figure 1 shows the distribution of profits reported abroad in the same 10 jurisdictions displayed in *Table 1.* The distribution is divided into two groups—one that includes the seven tax-preferred jurisdictions and another that is comprised of the three non-tax-preferred jurisdictions. The tax-preferred jurisdictions accounted for 50% of all profits reported as being earned outside the United States, in comparison to the 15% being reported in the three non-tax-preferred jurisdictions. At first glance, the fact that the seven tax-preferred jurisdictions are responsible for a larger share of reported profits may not seem surprising—a larger number of countries should account for a larger share of profits. But consider that the combined economic size of the tax-preferred group (as measured by GDP) is less than one-half that of the non-tax-preferred group ($2.23 trillion to $4.86 trillion).[17]

Figure 2 displays the share of workers hired and the share of property, plant, and equipment owned by American companies outside of the United States in both country groups. Comparing where American firms report profits (*Figure 1*) with where they have a physical presence as measured by the location of their employees and tangible capital indicates a disconnect between the two. While accounting for 50% of reported profits reported worldwide, 5% of employees and 11% of property can be attributed to the tax-preferred country group. In contrast, the three nontax-preferred countries of Canada, Norway, and the United Kingdom account for 20% of employees and 29% of property held by American MNCs worldwide.

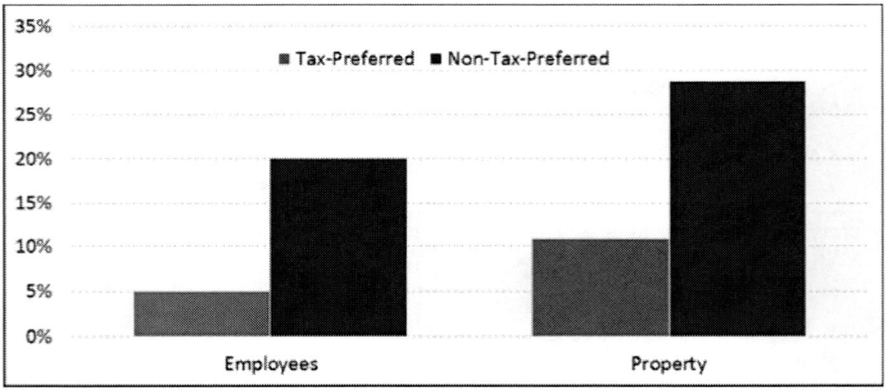

Source: CRS analysis of U.S. Bureau of Economic Analysis, Outward Activities of Multinational Enterprises: Operations of U.S. Parent Companies and Their Foreign Affiliates, Preliminary 2012 Statistics.

Notes: Profits are measured as net income plus foreign taxes paid. The tax-preferred group includes Bermuda, Ireland, Luxembourg, Netherlands, Singapore, Switzerland, and the U.K. Caribbean Islands. The non-taxpreferred group includes Canada, Norway, and the United Kingdom. Tax-Preferred is indicated by the left bar for Employees and Property and Non-Tax Preferred is indicated by the right bar for Employees and Property.

Figure 2. Employment and Property in Top-10 Profit Jurisdiction Groups as a Percentage of Foreign Employment and Investment of American MNCs (2012).

U.S. Foreign Direct Investment by Country

Data on the foreign direct investment (FDI) behavior of American MNCs can also shed some light on possible profit-shifting activity. FDI generally involves a multinational corporation's investment in its foreign subsidiaries.[18] There are a number of types of investments that can be categorized as FDI and not all of them are associated with profit shifting. For example, investments in real physical capital such as production plants and equipment are counted as FDI. At the same time, FDI also captures financial flows within a company group such as reinvested earnings and intra-company loans that may or may not be supporting real capital investment. It is these financial flows that cannot be tied to corresponding real investment that economists believe may be an indication of profit shifting.

To qualify as FDI, the parent corporation must have an ownership and controlling stake in the foreign entity it is investing in. Currently, the BEA and other international statistical agencies (e.g., International Monetary Fund) require that the domestic parent hold a minimum 10% ownership interest in the foreign "affiliate" to categorize an investment as FDI.[19] The ownership of the foreign affiliate by the domestic parent can be either direct or indirect. An example of indirect ownership would be if the American parent established a foreign holding company which in turn owned several foreign affiliates. In this case, the American parent would still be considered to hold an FDI position in the countries where the foreign affiliates were located. Thus, FDI activity in particular countries could be indicative of funds being channeled through intermediate firms within a holding company group. Tax planning is one of the possible motivations for this corporate structure.

Shown in *Figure 3* are the 10 countries with the largest positions of U.S. FDI. American MNCs are reporting a significant share of their FDI as occurring in tax-preferred countries. The seven tax-preferred countries—Netherlands, Luxembourg, Bermuda, Ireland, United Kingdom Caribbean Islands, Singapore, and Switzerland—accounted for 47% of the FDI positions of American companies, compared to 24% for the three larger industrialized nations of the United Kingdom, Canada, and Australia. Perhaps most interesting is that the Netherlands, while only a fraction of the economic size, holds more American FDI than Australia, Canada, and the United Kingdom.[20] FDI flow data (or change in FDI over a given point of time) show similar type patterns.[21]

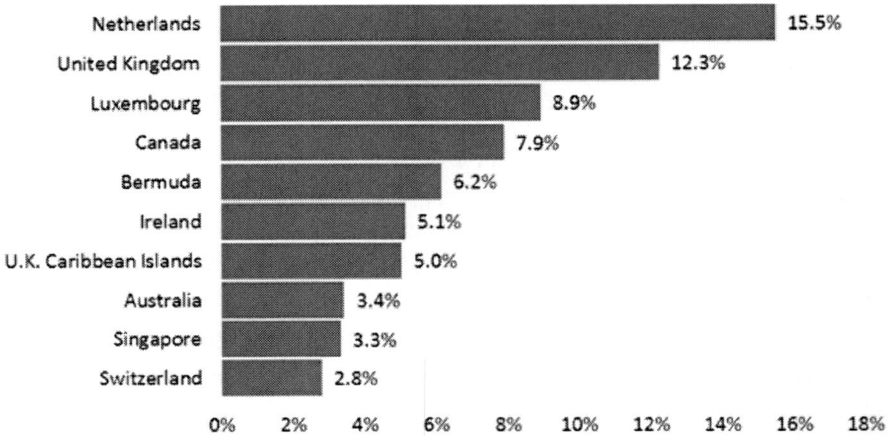

Source: CRS analysis of U.S. Bureau of Economic Analysis, U.S. Direct Investment Abroad: Balance of Payments and Direct Investment Position Data.

Figure 3. U.S. FDI Positions as a Percentage of Total U.S FDI Positions Held Abroad, by Country (2013).

U.S. Foreign Direct Investment Held Through Holding Companies

An increasingly popular way American companies have been structuring their operations and foreign investments is through the use of holding companies. In its simplest form, a holding company is an entity established to own the securities and assets of other companies.[22] The companies under the umbrella of a holding company can be located anywhere in the world. The holding company, in turn, is owned by a U.S. parent that is then deemed to have an indirect ownership or investment interest in the jurisdiction where the holding company's subordinates are located. *Figure 4* shows that over the last 30 years, the share of U.S. FDI owned through holding companies has increased from 9.4% to 46.2%.

Holding companies offer two significant advantages. First, organizing a group of subsidiaries under the umbrella of a holding company can allow for the streamlining of management, operations, financing, and leasing agreements which can increase business efficiency, lower costs, and boost profitability. Second, holding companies present a number of tax minimization opportunities.

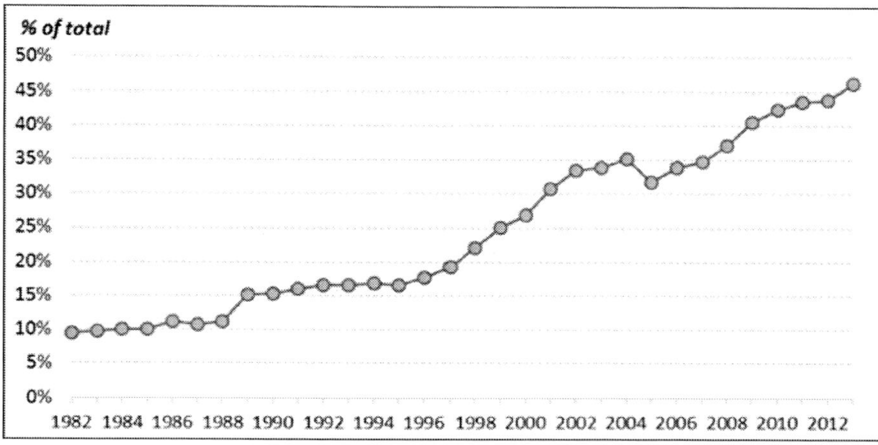

Source: CRS analysis of U.S. Bureau of Economic Analysis, U.S. Direct Investment Abroad: Balance of Payments and Direct Investment Position Data.

Figure 4. Share of Direct Investment Position Held Through Holding Companies (2013).

For example, if a U.S. corporation owns its foreign subsidiaries through a foreign holding company instead of directly, it becomes possible to transfer funds from one subsidiary to another without triggering U.S. tax by using the holding company as the intermediary in the transfer. Another example involves placing valuable intellectual property (IP) with a foreign holding company located in a low-tax jurisdiction and then licensing the IP to other subsidiaries in higher-tax jurisdictions. This results in a deductible royalty payment in the high-tax jurisdictions and income in the low-tax jurisdiction. Numerous other examples exist as to how holding companies fit into the profit shifting picture.[23]

Current data limitations prevent definitively determining whether multinational companies are increasingly using the holding-company structure for non-tax business reasons or to minimize taxes. Still, it is possible to look for anomalies that may be suggestive of why holding-company use is on the rise. Shown in *Figure 5* are the 10 most favored locations through which U.S. outward FDI is held via holding companies. In 2013, the amount of the U.S. FDI position abroad that was held through holding companies was approximately $2.2 trillion. Of that $2.2 trillion, 68% (or $1.5 trillion) was attributable to the seven tax-haven or tax-preferred locations of the Netherlands (27%), Luxembourg (16%), Bermuda (9%), Ireland (5%), the U.K. Caribbean Islands (5%), Singapore (4%), and Switzerland (2%). In contrast, the three traditional economies of the United Kingdom, Australia, and Germany collectively accounted for 14% of the U.S. FDI position abroad that was held through holding-company structures.

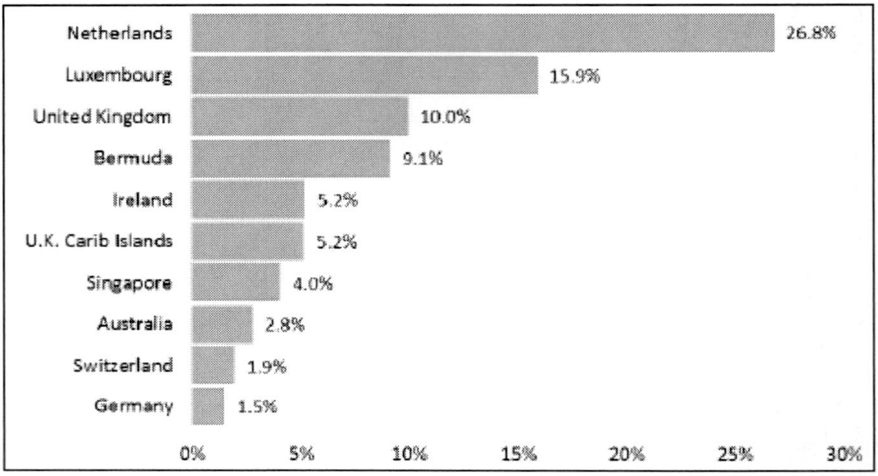

Source: CRS analysis of U.S. Bureau of Economic Analysis, U.S. Direct Investment Abroad: Balance of Payments and Direct Investment Position Data.

Figure 5. Share of Direct Investment Position Held Through Holding Companies, by Country (2013).

Indications of Worldwide Profit Shifting

Data from the International Monetary Fund (IMF) suggest that corporate profit shifting is not solely a U.S. issue. As indication of this, consider a comparison of foreign investment into the 10 largest economies and the 10 most popular investment destinations. *Figure 6* displays the inward FDI positions (that is, investments in each country from the rest of the world) as a percentage of GDP for the 10 largest economies.[24] On average the 10 largest economies in the world have an inward FDI position equal to 25% of their economies. Japan has the smallest FDI position (4% of GDP), while the U.K. has the largest (63% of GDP). The United States, with the largest economy, has an inward FDI position equal to 17% of GDP.

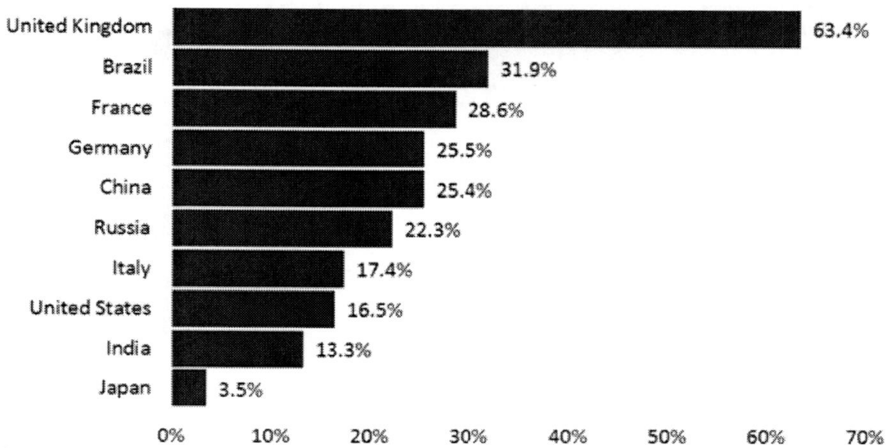

Source: CRS Analysis of IMF, World Economic Outlook Database, April 2014.

Figure 6. Inward FDI Position in10 Largest Economies as a Percentage of GDP (IMF, 2013).

In comparison, *Figure 7* shows the inward FDI positions of the 10 most popular direct investment destinations. Again, these FDI positions are the result of investment flowing in from the rest of the world. Two features of the data are immediately apparent. First, aside from Mongolia (where mining operations have attracted capital), the most popular direct investment destinations are all tax-haven or tax-preferred countries.[25] Second, the amount of investment into these countries far exceeds investment in the 10 largest economies. For example, the countries in *Figure 7* have an average inward FDI position equal to 961% the size of their economies. The least popular tax-preferred country in the group, Ireland, had an FDI position equal to 156% of GDP, which is more than twice that of the United Kingdom (see *Figure 6*). Luxembourg had the largest FDI position (5,434% of GDP).

The stock of FDI in the economies displayed in *Figure 7* is still notable without adjusting for countries' size. The Netherlands, for example, has a larger absolute inward FDI position ($4.3 trillion) than the largest economy in the world, the United States ($2.8 trillion). Luxembourg follows close behind with a $3.3 trillion inward FDI position. Combined, the Netherlands and Luxembourg account for 27% of worldwide inward FDI positions, which is more than the two largest economies in the world—the United States and China—which account for 18% combined.

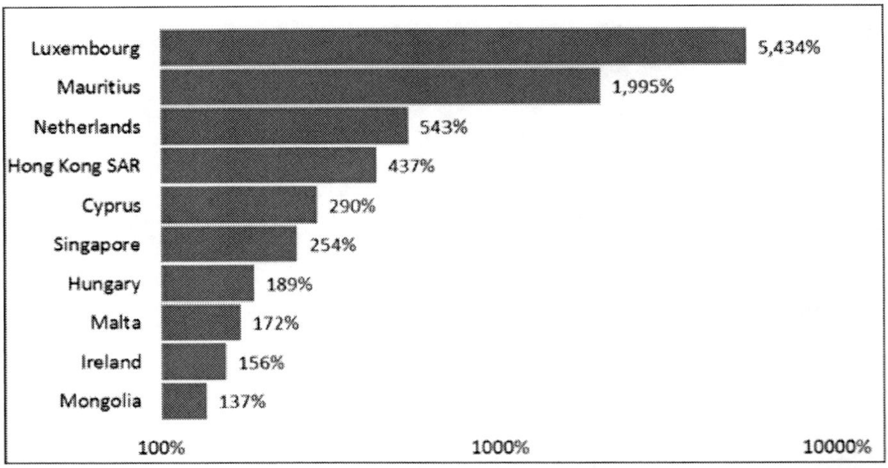

Source: CRS Analysis of IMF, World Economic Outlook Database, April 2014.

Notes: The data are graphed on a log-scale to accommodate the large range of values in a single graph. FDI data for Ireland and Malta are from 2012, as the data for 2013 were missing for these two countries.

Figure 7. Inward FDI Position In10 Most Popular Investment Destinations as a Percentage of GDP, Log-Scale (IMF, 2013).

The United Nations (U.N.) compiles data similar to the IMF. While differences in methodology, measurement issues, and countries covered by each group lead to discrepancies between the two datasets, both paint the same general picture; there is a disproportionate amount of FDI being reported in tax-haven and tax-preferred countries. *Figure 8* displays the 10 countries with the highest inward FDI postion to GDP ratios as reported by the U.N. in 2013. The British Virgin Islands has the largest inward FDI position, equal to 50,513% of GDP, followed by the Cayman Islands (4,708%), Hong Kong (524%), and the Marshall Islands (503%).

A final indication that profit shifting may be occuring can be found by looking at how much investment is funneled through special purpose entities (SPEs). According to the OECD,

> Examples [of SPEs] are financing subsidiaries, conduits, holding companies, shell companies, shelf companies and brass-plate companies. Although there is no universal definition of SPEs, they do share a number of features. They are all legal entities that have little or no employment, or operations, or physical presence in the jurisdication in which they are created by their parent enterprises which are typically located in other jurisdictions

(economies). They are often used as devices to raise capital or to hold assets and liabilities and usually do not undertake significant production.[26]

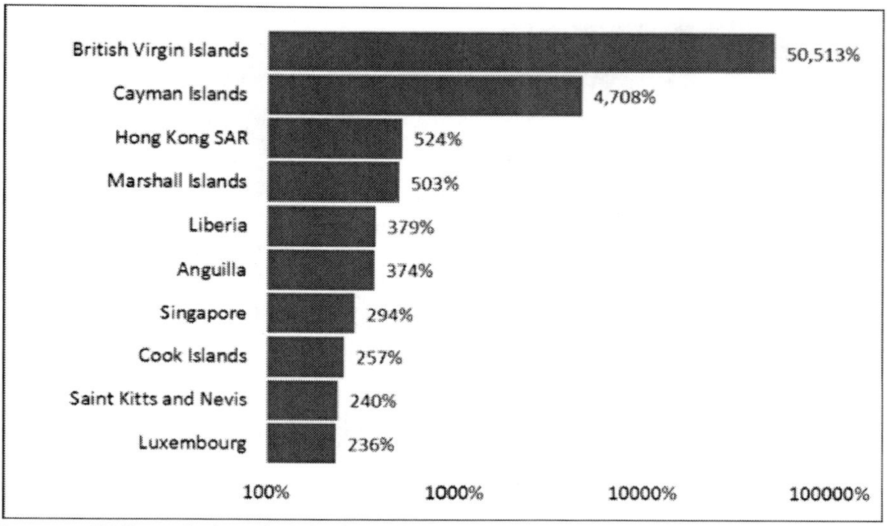

Source: CRS analysis of United Nations Conference on Trade and Development Statistics.

Notes: The data are graphed on a log-scale to accommodate the large range of values in a single graph. GDP figure for British Virgin Islands is from 2012.

Figure 8. Inward FDI Position in10 Most Popular Investment Destinations as a Percentage of GDP, Log-Scale (U.N., 2013).

Data on the use of SPEs are scarce. The OECD, however, does publish data on the inward FDI positions of the Netherlands and Luxembourg that are broken down into investment held through SPEs and non-SPEs. In 2013, the total inward FDI stock held via SPEs in Luxembourg and the Netherlands was $3.1 trillion and $3.9 trillion, respectively, both of which are larger than the total inward FDI stock of the United States. As *Figure 9* shows, 83% ($3.2 trillion) of the inward FDI position in the Netherlands is held through SPEs. For Luxembourg the share is even higher; 96% of its inward FDI position is held through SPEs.

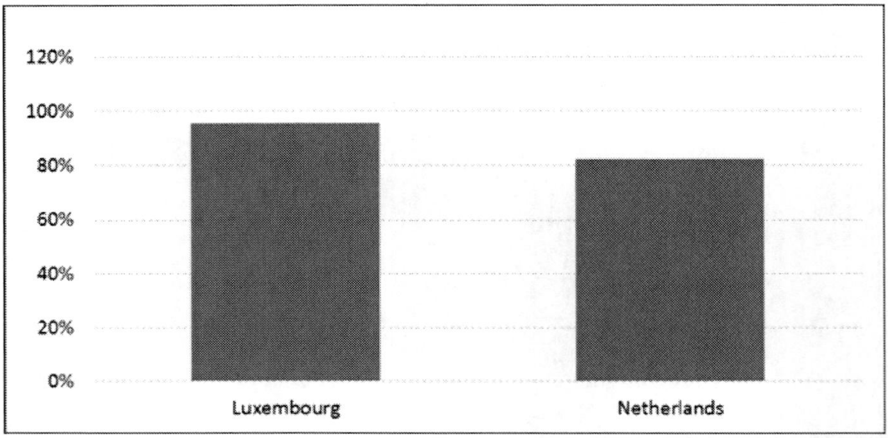

Source: CRS analysis of OECD Foreign Direct Investment (FDI) Statistics, FDI series from 1990 to Q4 2013.

Figure 9. Share of Total Inward FDI Position Held Through Special Purpose Entities (2013).

POLICY OPTIONS AND CONSIDERATIONS FOR REDUCING PROFIT SHIFTING

The debate over reducing profit shifting and reforming the international tax system may involve a number of policy considerations and tradeoffs. Proposals thus far have included moving closer toward a pure-form worldwide system, moving closer toward a pure-form territorial system, adopting a new approach such as a minimum tax or formula apportionment, or modifying the current system's rules and structure. There is also on the horizon the completion of OECD's Base Erosion and Profit Shifting (BEPS) initiative. The remainder of this report discusses these considerations generally.

Worldwide vs. Territorial Taxation

There have been calls for the United States to change its approach to taxing American MNCs. The United States currently follows what roughly approximates the so-called "worldwide" approach to taxation. While the United States generally follows this approach, corporations are typically allowed to defer paying taxes on income earned abroad until that income is brought home, or repatriated, in the form of a dividend payment to the U.S. parent. Additionally, foreign taxes paid in one country may be used to offset income earned in other countries via a process known as cross-crediting. These two features—deferral and cross-crediting—result in the current system straying away from the worldwide approach and into a hybrid system with both worldwide and territorial system features. Where exactly on the spectrum between worldwide and territorial taxation the current system lies is not precisely known. The general implications of moving closer toward either system are discussed below.

Move Closer Toward Worldwide Taxation

If the United States were to transition toward a more pure-form worldwide system, the most straightforward way to do this would be to eliminate deferral while still allowing a credit for foreign taxes paid. Such an approach would result in U.S. investments being taxed at the same total tax rate (foreign plus U.S.), regardless of where investments were made.[27] As a result, investment decisions would be made based on real economic returns and not on any differential between U.S. and foreign tax rates. This, in turn, would lead U.S. corporations to allocate capital to its most productive use in the world economy. Additionally, corporations would largely have no incentive to shift profits or to accumulate large sums of cash overseas (like the current system incentivizes firms to do) because all earnings would be taxed currently.

A reduction in the incentive to shift profits as the result of a purer-form worldwide system would also likely reduce complexity in the administration of the tax system because many tax strategies would be rendered useless. A pure-form-type system would still likely require that income and costs be allocated between domestic and foreign activities for purposes of the foreign tax credit. If the movement to a more worldwide system was accompanied by a per-country foreign tax credit limit (to eliminate cross-crediting), however, then U.S. corporations would have to allocate income and expenses between domestic and foreign activities *and* allocate income and expenses between affiliated foreign subsidiaries. To the extent that firms were in an excess credit position (had credits they could not use because of the foreign tax credit limit), there would be an incentive to shift profits to lower-tax countries. Without the ability to defer income, however, excess credits would likely be reduced.

There are concerns over moving toward a more pure-form worldwide tax system. Without the proper safeguards in place, it is likely that a true worldwide tax system would encourage corporations to shed their U.S. corporate charter by reincorporating abroad via a process known as "inversion." Several high profile U.S. companies expressed interest in inverting under the current hybrid system in early and mid-2014. In response, Treasury released a notice of regulatory changes that would further restrict the ability to invert and has indicated that additional actions are possible. Legislation was also introduced in Congress that would modify current laws meant to curb the practice, although nothing was enacted.[28] The recent regulatory changes and proposed legislative changes would likely need to be strengthened to prevent inversions under a pure worldwide system.[29]

Concern has also been expressed that moving from the current hybrid system to a true worldwide system would reduce America's international competitive position. Using "competition" as an evaluation criterion is problematic because generally it is not well defined in the context of international tax policy, and often times the "competitive" concepts that are used are at odds with each other.[30] For example, does increasing America's competitive position call for tax policies that promote the flow of U.S. capital (and therefore business operations and jobs) abroad to better compete in international markets? Or does it call for policies that reduce the flow of capital (and therefore business operations and jobs) abroad so that it remains in the United States and can be put to use domestically? There is an argument that these two objectives are not at odds with each other, and that promoting increased foreign investment and employment complements increased domestic investment and employment.[31] There is not conclusive evidence to support this argument.

Additionally, it is important to understand that countries do not compete with each other in an economic sense. Competition implies a zero-sum game with winners and losers. But enhanced economic well-being in one country generally does not reduce economic opportunities in other countries. Instead, countries *trade* with each other. When countries specialize in what they have a comparative advantage at producing and trade for what they have a comparative disadvantage at producing, they are able to produce more together than in isolation. Greater production leads to more product variety, lower consumer prices, and greater average incomes.[32] For these reasons, economists typically question whether "competitiveness" makes sense as a tax policy objective for a country. For economists, the typical objective is economic efficiency, or the optimal allocation of limited resources.

Move Closer Toward Territorial Taxation

If the United States were to transition toward a more pure-form of a territorial system it would forgo taxing income earned outside its borders. This change would result in U.S. investments being taxed at the rates that exist where the investments are made. As a result, investment decisions would no longer be based solely on real economic returns, but on after-tax returns that would vary country by country. This variation, in turn, would lead U.S. corporations to allocate more investment to lower-tax countries than they otherwise would. Another feature of a territorial-based system would be that tax policy would no longer affect corporations' decisions to repatriate income because there would be no tax consequence for doing so. Recall that a pure worldwide system would also remove the influence of taxes on the repatriation decision, but in that case, it would be because taxes were unavoidable and not because repatriation would be tax-free.

It is argued that relative to the current hybrid system, a more territorial system would enhance the competitiveness of U.S. firms relative to their foreign competitors. Again, however, economists are typically skeptical of using competition criteria when evaluating international tax policy, whether it is comparing a territorial system with the current system or with a true worldwide system. Still, the effective U.S. tax burden on foreign earned income is already argued by some analysts to be quite low because of the ability to shift income to low-tax countries, suggesting that the current system may not be inhibiting the overseas operations of American MNCs.[33]

A territorial system raises some of the same concerns that the current system does regarding profit shifting. Specifically, profit shifting could increase under a territorial system without the proper anti-abuse provisions in place. With a territorial system, income earned abroad would be exempt from U.S. tax. MNCs would therefore have an incentive to attribute as much income as possible to operations outside the United States. Anti-abuse provisions particularly focused on the transfer of intangible assets (patents, intellectual property, etc.) out of the United States may be the most useful at curbing profit shifting under a territorial system.

Does the Distinction Matter?

There is the issue of whether the distinction between worldwide and territorial systems is even relevant for current policy debates.[34] Among the major economies, no country has either a pure worldwide or territorial system—they are all hybrid systems. The problem then becomes one of degree and depends on the specific differences in each country's international tax regime. For example, a country typically classified as having a worldwide-based system could actually tax foreign source income at a lower effective rate than a country that is typically classified as having a territorial system. One possible way this could arise is if the worldwide-based country allows deferral for most types of income, and the territorial-based country has in place effective base erosion provisions. Which system is preferable in this situation is not clear.

Problems can also arise when attempting to empirically analyze or compare worldwide and territorial systems as two distinct country groups. Labeling a system as worldwide or territorial without considering where on the "spectrum" it lies is too simplistic and can lead to mislabeling. This mislabeling, in turn, can lead to questionable empirical results when comparing groups of countries labeled as "worldwide" and "territorial" because the countries within the groups are themselves quite heterogeneous. It may be better to stick to pairwise comparison so that the nuances of the two systems can be better accounted for.

Adopt a Minimum Tax

A worldwide minimum tax could potentially allow for some balance to be struck between multinational corporations' concerns over tax burdens and governments' concerns over profit shifting.[35] With a minimum tax, income earned in countries with a tax rate below a specified threshold would be subject to immediate U.S. taxation at the threshold tax rate. Income earned in countries with a tax rate above the threshold would be exempt from U.S. tax or eligible for deferral. Typically, a credit would be allowed for foreign taxes paid, but the credit would be calculated on a country-by-country basis to prevent cross-crediting.

An example may be useful. Say that the United States set a minimum tax threshold of 20% of net income. If a corporation where to report $100 million of income as being earned in a country with a tax rate of 15%, the corporation would then be subject to a 20% U.S. tax in the year the income was earned. However, the United States would credit the corporation for the 15% in taxes paid abroad, leaving the company with a residual U.S. tax of 5%. The foreign tax credit prevents double taxation of income and also ensures that the firm's total tax rate is no greater than 20% (15% to the foreign country plus 5% to the United States). The minimum tax could also apply only to particular types of income, such as passive income or income associated with intellectual property.

Several proposals to install a minimum tax have been offered in recent years. In the 112th Congress, Senator Enzi introduced S. 2091, which would have enacted a minimum tax equal to half the top U.S. corporate rate, but would have exempted active business income. Former Senate Finance Committee Chairman Max Baucus's tax reform discussion draft, published in November 2013, also included several options for imposing a minimum tax.[36] Senator Baucus never introduced formal legislative language so it is not clear exactly how the tax would have been structured, or to what income it would have applied. Former Ways and Means Chairman Dave Camp's Tax Reform Act of 2014 (H.R. 1) included a minimum tax that ranged from between 12.5% to 25% depending on the type of income.[37] Most recently, the President's FY2016 budget includes a proposed 19% minimum tax on American corporations' overseas income.[38]

The minimum tax approach could have some undesirable features depending on its design.[39] If the minimum tax only applied to low-tax-rate countries it could still leave an incentive to shift profits to countries with a tax rate just above the minimum tax. For example, if the minimum tax only applied to countries with a tax rate of 10% or lower, profits could still be shifted to Ireland which has a 12.5% tax rate without triggering the tax. This problem could be avoided or at least mitigated by setting the minimum tax rate appropriately high enough (for example, at the average of the countries not considered tax havens). The problem would also be avoided by imposing an overall minimum worldwide tax with a credit for taxes paid.

Second, there is concern that designing a minimum tax may be too complex.[40] For example, would it be each country's statutory tax rate or each company's effective tax rate that would be subject to the minimum threshold? If it were the latter, how would scenarios involving companies in a relatively high-tax country that experiences large losses in a year (lowering their effective tax rate) be handled? And third, concern has been expressed that a minimum tax is really a patchwork structure that is not consistent with either a territorial or worldwide system. The same argument, however, can be made about the current U.S. international tax system.

Adopt Formula Apportionment

Another option that has been suggested that could reduce profit shifting is the adoption of a formula apportionment approach to taxation. The current system requires U.S. corporations to price transactions between affiliated companies to determine the allocation of income and expenses. This provides an opportunity to shift profits to low-tax countries. An alternative would be to pool profits earned around the world and then allow countries to tax a share of the total profits, eliminating the need for transfer pricing. The share each country could tax would be determined by a formula that measures real business activity conducted in each country.

To understand how formula apportionment works, it may help to consider an example of a sales-based approach. Under this method, if a U.S. company earned $100 million of profits worldwide and 60% of its sales occurred domestically, then the United States would have the right to tax $60 million ($100 million multiplied by 60%). The remaining $40 million could be subject to taxation in the jurisdictions where the 40% of foreign sales occurred. More realistically, the formula used to apportion profits might depend on more than just sales, such as the location of assets and employees. In this case, known as a multi-factor formula, taxable profits would be determined by the weighted average of factor activity occurring in each country. For example, if a company had 60% of its sales, 30% of its assets, and 25% of its employees in the United States, then the share of income that would be taxable in the United States would be $100 million multiplied by (0.6+0.3+0.25)/3, or $38.3 million.[41]

There is currently a debate among economists over desirability of switching to a formula apportionment regime and its ability to reduce profit shifting.[42] If the apportionment formula can be easily manipulated then its impact on profit shifting may be limited. It has been argued that a sales-based formula would be less susceptible to manipulation. At the same time, it has been argued that without extensive recordkeeping or a tracking system, nothing would stop an MNC from setting up a chain of subsidiaries in low-tax countries to which intermediate components are sold on their way to their final destination, which could be a high-tax country. Determining how those intermediate sales are to be treated in the allocation formula could be difficult, or at least increase the administrative complexity of the approach. Alternatively, a U.S. MNC could enter into a sales contract with an unrelated foreign distributer who is based in a low-tax country. Again, the sales to the distributer would seem to dictate that the MNC's profits should be allocated to the low-tax location of its distributer. There has been, however, legislative and regulatory language proposed by at least one tax practitioner that is aimed at addressing these concerns.[43]

The increasing role of intangible assets (patents, trademarks, copyrights, etc.) may also limit a formula apportionment regime's capacity to reduce profit shifting. For example, a sales-based approach would generally result in some share of taxable income being apportioned to foreign locations when that income arguably should be taxable in the United States since that is where the initial R&D investment was made. Additionally, to the extent that the investment was subsidized by the U.S. government via the tax code or federal funding (e.g., NSF grants, SBA loans, etc.) it could be argued that the associated income should be taxable in the United States. A multi-factor formula that incorporated assets may not fare much better given the difficulty of valuing intangible assets. Still, formula apportionment may result in more income being subject to tax in more jurisdictions than currently occurs.

Formula apportionment may also require international cooperation. It is possible that if countries unilaterally establish a formula-apportionment-type system that some income could either face no taxation or double taxation. The reason for this is differences in tax systems and taxable bases across countries. Harmonizing tax systems so that they mirrored each other as closely as possible would likely mitigate the risk of lapses or redundancies in the worldwide tax system.

Modify Subpart F Rules

In contrast to a minimum tax, which targets the income earned in particular low-tax countries, Congress could target the types of income firms use to shift money to tax havens. This was the intent of the Subpart F rules that were enacted to prevent deferral of highly fungible income that can be more easily shifted.[44] Since 1997, however, there has existed a temporary "active financing income" exception to the Subpart F rules.[45] The active financing exception allows deferral for certain types of passive income earned by American corporations that operate banking, financing, and insurance lines of business abroad, even if their primary line of business is quite different. On the one hand, there is the argument that there are real economic reasons for keeping this income abroad and that transactions involving active financing income are not necessarily for tax avoidance purposes. On the other hand, it could be argued that passive income is passive income, regardless of the underlying line of business. Nonetheless, active financing income earned through the end of 2014 qualified for deferral and in recent years has only been taxed when it is repatriated to the United States. Congress could choose to modify the active financing exception if it were to extend the provision again for 2015, or allow it to remain expired if Congress believes the exception is used more to avoid taxes than to finance real operations.

Another option would be to expand the definition of Subpart F income. For example, the President's FY2015 and FY2016 budgets both included an expanded definition of Subpart F income that would include "foreign base company digital income," or income derived from selling or licensing digital products and services.[46] Expanding the definition of Subpart F income to encompass more income related to intangible assets may help curb profit shifting; a significant share of profit shifting is believed to be associated with intangible assets.

Reduce Corporate Tax Rates

One topic that has been part of nearly every debate regarding corporate tax reform has been the 35% top statutory corporate tax rate. Reducing this rate would decrease the incentive to shift profits by reducing the tax savings from such behavior. Companies profit shift to take advantage of the differential between the U.S. tax rate and rates in low-tax countries. By reducing this discrepancy, the incentive to shift profits would be reduced as well. Note, however, that reducing the U.S. tax rate to within the range typically suggested, 25% to 28%, would still leave the United States as a high-tax country relative to tax havens, implying that the incentive to profit shift would remain. A reduction in the top tax rate may also reduce federal revenue because of lower tax rates being applied to corporate net income.[47] Combining a rate reduction with a broadening of the corporate tax base and strong anti-base erosion provisions would help to offset any revenue loss.[48]

The OECD's BEPS Project

At the request of the G20 finance ministers, the OECD has initiated the development of an Action Plan on Base Erosion and Profit Shifting. The goal is to develop 15 detailed actions governments can take that will reduce *double non-taxation* of corporate and individual income—a situation where profit shifting gives rise to so-called "stateless" or "homeless" income—and prevent the *double taxation* of income. If successful, the Action Plan should also lead to a more coherent and transparent international tax system. Some of the actions will require coordination and information sharing between governments, and potentially the amendment of over 3,000 existing tax treaties.[49] As a result, success of the Action Plan will likely depend on widespread participation by G-20 and OECD member countries as well as nonmember countries.

The OECD set three deadlines for producing "deliverables" consisting initially of reports and draft rules, and culminating with the finalized 15-point Action Plan. The first set of deliverables was presented to and endorsed by the G20 finance ministers on time in September 2014. It was later endorsed by the G20 heads of government at the Brisbane Summit in November 2014. The second set of deliverables is scheduled for September 2015, and the third set of deliverables, which will include the final Action Plan, is scheduled for December 2015. *Appendix A* provides more details on the Action Plan and its current status.[50]

The OECD has been careful to stress that many of the strategies used by multinational corporations are likely legal.[51] The Director of the OECD's Centre for Tax Policy and Administration, Pascal Saint-Amans, said in a 2013 interview, "What we say at the OECD, [is] that we shouldn't put the blame on the business. The business and the companies are doing their job, which is to plan their taxes, to do aggressive tax planning. It can be more or less aggressive, sometimes it's too aggressive, but basically this is legal."[52] Thus, for the most part, the BEPS project does not appear to be driven primarily by concerns over the legality of corporate tax planning.

Instead, the OECD has argued that BEPS is important for three other reasons.[53] First, the ability of multinational corporations to artificially lower their taxes gives them a competitive advantage over companies that primarily operate in their home market. Second, profit shifting and base erosion distort investment by altering the relative rates of return across locations. An efficient tax system would direct capital to locations based on real economic returns. Instead, profit shifting can result in more capital investment in jurisdictions with a lower economic return but a higher after-tax return because of tax differentials. And third, the OECD argues BEPS is important based on fairness concerns. If multinational corporations have the means to avoid or reduce taxes, and other taxpayers (including individuals) do not, then it may create the perception that the tax system is unfair. Furthermore, tax avoidance by some may encourage tax avoidance by others.

There are a number of reasons why Congress may want to consider the implication of the BEPS Action Plan even though it is still being formalized. The objective of the OECD's project is to build consensus among countries on a more coherent and transparent international tax system. So far, the Treasury Department has been the primary representative of the United States in BEPS-related negotiations and meetings, although the business community has also been actively involved in providing feedback on proposed rules. In the end, however, several of the proposed actions may require modification of existing tax treaties.[54] The Senate would need to ratify any tax treaty modifications. Treaty modification and negotiations under the Action Plan framework may suggest a multilateral approach which is different than the bilateral approach the United States traditionally has followed for tax treaties. It is unclear at this point if particular tax laws would be subject to change too. Harmonization of tax bases and anti-abuse policies could potentially call for modification to the IRC, which would require congressional approval.

Additionally, even if the U.S. does not implement any of the proposed actions, U.S. multinationals will likely still be impacted.[55] For example, some countries have already taken unilateral actions to preserve their tax bases and there is concern more may follow, which could impact U.S. multinationals.[56] While unilateral action may sound encouraging, it runs contrary to the OECD's goal of creating a coordinated, multilateral, and transpartent international tax regime. The U.K.'s diverted profits tax proposal has been identified as one such example. The tax, which went into effect on April 1, 2015, subjects income deemed to have been articifially shifted out of the U.K. to a 25% tax. The tax is aimed at curbing profit shifting by MNCs, particularly American MNCs with U.K. operations, with the tax being referred to by some as the "Google tax."[57]

Once the Action Plan is finalized and adopted, American MNCs could also be subject to some of its base erosion rules even if the U.S. does not adopt the rules. For example, a country that adopts the BEPS country-by-country reporting standards could require U.S. companies to report detailed operating information for each country they operate in to that country's tax authority so that the tax authority can determine whether their domestic tax base is being eroded by profit shifting. It has been pointed out by practioners that this in turn, could result in non-adopting countries (including the U.S.) requesting such information for their own purposes (since they know the firm has already had to compile it). Likewise, if other countries adopt the OECD's suggestions for targeting hybrid mistmatch arrangements, or the taxation of income associated with intangible assets, American multinationals may find it more difficult to shift profits regardless if the U.S. adopts such recommendations.[58]

Lastly, concerns exist over the OECD's approach. For example, some commentators have raised the posibility that in an attempt to reduce BEPS, the OECD's efforts may end up stifling trade and international investment.[59] To the extent this happens, the extra revenue governments collect as the result of reduced profit shifting may not be enough to compensate for the decline in economic activity.

APPENDIX A. OECD'S BEPS ACTION PLAN STATUS

The OECD set three deadlines for producing "deliverables" leading to the finalized proposed Action Plan: September 2014, September 2015 and December 2015. The first set of deliverables was presented to and endorsed by the G20 Finance Ministers on time in September 2014. They were later endorsed by the G20 heads of government at the Brisbane Summit in November 2014. The first set of deliverables was comprised of the following items:[60]

1. A report identifying tax challenges raised by the digital economy and the necessary actions to address them (Action 1)
2. Recommended rules for dealing with hybrid mismatch arrangements (Action 2)
3. A report reviewing member country regimes in order to counter harmful tax practices by increasing transparency (Action 5)
4. Recommended rules regarding the design of domestic and tax treaty measures to prevent abuse of tax treaties (Action 6)
5. Recommended rules for transfer pricing involving intangibles (Action 8)
6. Recommended rules for transfer pricing in relation to country-by-country documentation requirements (Action 13)
7. A report on the development of a multilateral, as opposed to a bilateral, mechanism to implement BEPS measures, particularly with regard to treaty modification (Action 15)

According to the OECD, the following deliverables (as well as the completed Action Plan) are on schedule. The remaining deliverables include the following:

September 2015

8. Recommendations regarding the design of domestic rules to strengthen Controlled Foreign Companies (CFC) Rules (Action 3)
9. Recommendations regarding the design of domestic rules to limit base erosion via interest deductions and other financial payments (Action 4)
10. Strategy to expand participation to non-OECD members to counter harmful tax practices more effectively (Action 5)

11. Tax treaty measures to prevent the artificial avoidance of permanent establishment status (Action 7)
12. Changes to the transfer pricing rules in relation to risks and capital, and other high-risk transactions (Actions 9 and 10)
13. Recommendations regarding data on BEPS to be collected and methodologies to analyze them (Action 11)
14. Recommendations regarding the design of domestic rules to require taxpayers to disclose their aggressive tax planning arrangements (Action 12)
15. Tax treaty measures to make dispute resolution mechanisms more effective (Action 14)

December 2015

16. Changes to the transfer pricing rules to limit base erosion via interest deductions and other financial payments (Action 4)
17. Revision of existing criteria to counter harmful tax practices more effectively (Action 5)
18. The development of a multilateral instrument (Action 15)
19. Completion of the full 15 item Action Plan

End Notes

1 For example, see Charles Duhigg and David Kocieniewski, "How Apple Sidesteps Billions in Taxes," The New York Times, April 28, 2012, p. A1; Jesse Drucker, "Google 2.4% Rate Shows How $60 Billion Lost to Tax Loopholes," Bloomberg, October 21, 2010, http://www.bloomberg.com/news/2010-10-21/google-2-4-rate-shows-how-60-billion-us-revenue-lost-to-tax-loopholes.html/; Jesse Drucker, "IRS Auditing How Google Shifted Profits Offshore to Avoid Taxes," Bloomberg, October 13, 2011, http://www.bloomberg.com/news/2011-10-13/irs-auditing-how-google-shiftedprofits-offshore-to-avoid-taxes.html; and Richard Rubin, "Profit Shifting: Moving to Cut U.S. Taxes," Bloomberg, February 18, 2015, BloombergQuickTake.

2 House of Commons, Committee Public Accounts, HM Revenue & Customs: Annual Report and Accounts 2011-12, Nineteenth Report of Session 2012-1, November 28, 2012, http://www.publications.parliament.uk/pa/cm201213/ cmselect/cmpubacc/716/716.pdf.

3 The Federal Government of Germany, "Speech by Federal Chancellor Angela Merkel to the OECD Conference," February 19, 2014, http://www.bundesregierung.de/Content/EN/Reden/2014/2014-02-19-oecd-merkel-paris_en.html.

4 "France will not tolerate tax avoidance, says Francois Hollande," The Telegraph, February 6, 2014, http://www.telegraph.co.uk/finance/personalfinance/tax/10622933/France-will-not-tolerate-tax-avoidance-saysFrancois-Hollande.html.

[5] For more information on the G20, see CRS Report R40977, The G-20 and International Economic Cooperation: Background and Implications for Congress, by Rebecca M. Nelson.

[6] "Tax haven" is not a precisely defined term, but in most usages it refers to a country—in many cases a small one— where nonresidents can save taxes by conducting various investments, transactions, and activities. Attributes that may make a country a successful tax haven include low or nonexistent tax rates applicable to foreigners; strict bank and financial secrecy laws; and a highly developed communications, financial, and legal infrastructure.

[7] The concepts discussed here are described in greater detail in CRS Report R41852, U.S. International Corporate Taxation: Basic Concepts and Policy Issues, by Mark P. Keightley and Jeffrey M. Stupak, and CRS Report RL34115, Reform of U.S. International Taxation: Alternatives, by Jane G. Gravelle.

[8] For a discussion of whether the distinction between worldwide and territorial systems is still valid, see Kimberly A. Clausing, "Beyond Territorial and Worldwide Systems of International Taxation," Working Paper, February 2015, at http://ssrn.com/ abstract= 2567952.

[9] Repatriation is technically accomplished via a dividend payment from a foreign subsidiary to its American parent corporation.

[10] The economic concept of the "time value of money" states that a dollar today is more valuable than a dollar in the future.

[11] A foreign subsidiary is a legal entity separate from its parent company, while a foreign branch is an extension of a domestic company.

[12] Specifically, the tax treatment of subpart F income may be found in Sections 951 to 956 of the IRC.

[13] A rule called "check-the-box" has undermined subpart F provisions by allowing foreign subsidiaries to make transactions between themselves, such as loans and royalty payments, which are not recognized as taxable transactions by law. With check-the-box a corporation can set up a foreign subsidiary that owns another foreign subsidiary. The company then "checks a box" on an IRS form choosing to have the lower-level subsidiary treated as a disregarded (fiscally transparent) company for tax purposes. Transactions between the two subsidiaries are then treated as if they are occurring within the same company, avoiding the subpart F anti-deferral rules.

[14] Sections 901 to 909 of the IRC define the foreign tax credit rules.

[15] For more information on tax havens, see CRS Report R40623, Tax Havens: International Tax Avoidance and Evasion, by Jane G. Gravelle.

[16] U.S. Energy Information Administration, Norway Analysis Brief, April 28, 2014, http://www.eia.gov/countries/ cab.cfm?fips=NO.

[17] Data come from the United Nations Conference on Trade and Development Statistics, 2013.

[18] The other major category for international capital flows is foreign portfolio investment which mainly involves individual investment in foreign securities.

[19] The U.S. parent must own at least 10% of the foreign company's voting securities if it is a corporation or an equivalent interest if the foreign company is unincorporated.

[20] The Dutch economy is 53% the size of Australia's, 44% the size of Canada's, and 32% the size of the U.K.'s according to data from the United Nations Conference on Trade and Development Statistics, 2013.

[21] FDI position data was used because they are less susceptible to year-to-year fluctuations.

[22] Marilyn Ibarra-Caton and Raymond J. Mataloni Jr., Direct Investment Positions for 2013: Country and Industry Detail, U.S. Bureau of Economic Analysis, Washington , DC, July

2014, p. 7, http://www.bea.gov/scb/pdf/2014/07%20July/0714_direct_investment_positions.pdf.

[23] For an accessible introduction to holding companies and tax strategies, see David Buss, David Hryck, and Robert Rothman, "International Tax Strategies," Taxes, April 2005.

[24] More precisely, the amount of investment from other countries that the IMF measures.

[25] The Netherlands and Hungary do not appear on the typical tax haven lists often cited, although many argue that they should. Again, however, since the definition of what constitutes a tax haven is not universally agreed upon, these countries can arguably be placed in the "tax-preferred" category at a minimum. For more countries over which there is similar debate, see CRS Report R40623, Tax Havens: International Tax Avoidance and Evasion, by Jane G. Gravelle.

[26] OECD, Addressing Base Erosion and Profit Shifting, 2013, p. 22, http://dx.doi.org/10.1787/9789264192744-en.

[27] To see this, consider a U.S. firm that must allocate investment between two locations. The first location, Country A, has a 15% tax rate, while the second location, Country B, has a 30% tax rate. Under a pure worldwide system, income earned in Country A would be subject to a 15% foreign tax, and then a residual 20% U.S. tax after claiming a credit for foreign taxes paid. The result is a total (foreign plus U.S.) tax of 35%. Income earned in Country B would be subject to a 20% foreign tax, and then a residual 15% U.S. tax also resulting in a total tax of 35%. Thus, under a pure worldwide system, the total tax rate in both countries is the same, and taxes have no effect on investment decisions.

[28] For more information on corporate inversions, including legislative proposals, see CRS Report R43568, Corporate Expatriation, Inversions, and Mergers: Tax Issues, by Donald J. Marples and Jane G. Gravelle.

[29] A detailed discussion about this subject is beyond the scope of this report and can involve intricate legal technicalities. For an introduction to this issue, see CRS Report R43568, Corporate Expatriation, Inversions, and Mergers: Tax Issues, by Donald J. Marples and Jane G. Gravelle.

[30] For a more in-depth discussion of this issue, see Jane G. Gravelle, "Does the Concept of Competitiveness Have Meaning in Formulating Corporate Tax Policy?" Tax Law Review, vol. 65 (2012), pp. 326-337.

[31] Mihir A. Desai, Fritz Foley, and James R. Hines, "Domestic Effects of the Foreign Activities of US Multinationals," American Economic Journal: Economic Policy, vol. 1, no. 1 (February 2009), pp. 181-203.

[32] British economist David Ricardo first formalized the idea of comparative advantage in his 1817 book titled On the Principles of Political Economy and Taxation.

[33] Edward D. Kleinbard, "Stateless Income's Challenge to Tax Policy," Tax Notes, September 5, 2011, pp. 1021-1042.

[34] The discussion here is based on Kimberly A. Clausing, "Beyond Territorial and Worldwide Systems of International Taxation," Working Paper, February 2015, http://ssrn.com/abstract=2567952.

[35] See, for example, Rosanne Altshuler and Harry Grubert, "Fixing the System: An Analysis of Alternative Proposals for the Reform of International Tax," National Tax Journal, vol. 66, no. 3 (September 2013), pp. 671-712.

[36] For more information on Senator Baucus's international tax reform discussion draft, see http://www.finance.senate.gov/newsroom/chairman/release/?id=f946a9f3-d296-42ad-bae4-bcf451b34b14. United States Senate Committee on Finance, "Baucus Unveils Proposal for

International Tax Reform," press release, November 19, 2013, http://www.finance.senate.gov/newsroom/chairman/release/?id=f946a9f3-d296-42ad-bae4- bcf451b34b14.

37 The specific minimum tax rates proposed were 12.5% on foreign base company sales income, 15% on foreign base company intangible income, and 25% on foreign base company income. For a summary of the relevant international tax provisions contained in H.R. 1, see U.S. Congress, Joint Committee on Taxation, Technical Explanation of the Tax Reform Act of 2014, A Discussion Draft of The Chairman of The House Committee on Ways and Means to Reform The Internal Revenue Code: Title IV—Participation Exemption System for the Taxation of Foreign Income, 113th Cong., 2nd sess., February 26, 2014, JCX-15-14.

38 For more information on the President's budget, see Department of the Treasury, General Explanations of the Administration's Fiscal Year 2016 Revenue Proposals, February 2015, http://www.treasury.gov/resource-center/taxpolicy/Documents/General-Explanations-FY2016.pdf.

39 A number of these concerns are expressed in Julie Martin "Minimum Tax on Multinationals Could Slow Profit Shifting," Tax Notes, March 19, 2012.

40 This concern has been expressed by Ed Kleinbard, Professor of Law, University of Southern California Gould School of Law. Reported in Julie Martin, "Minimum Tax on Multinationals Could Slow Profit Shifting," Tax Notes, March 19, 2012.

41 This is an example of an equal-weighted multi-factor formula. A more complex formula would give different weights to each factor.

42 For a sample of the ongoing debate in the literature, see Reuven S. Avi-Yonah and Kimberly A. Clausing, Reforming Corporate Taxation in a Global Economy: A proposal to Adopt Formulary Apportionment, Hamilton Project Discussion Paper, Brookings Institution, June 2007, http://www.brookings.edu/~/media/research/files/papers/2007/6/ corporatetaxes-clausing/200706clausing_aviyonah.pdf; Rosanne Altshuler and Harry Grubert, "Formula Apportionment: Is it better than the current system and are there better alternatives?" National Tax Journal , vol. 63, no. 4 (December 2010), pp. 1145-1184; Kimberly A. Clausing, Lessons for International Tax Reform from the U.S. State Experience under Formulary Apportionment, Working Paper, June 29, 2014, http://ssrn.com/ abstract=2359724; and J. Clifton Fleming Jr., Robert J. Peroni, and Stephen E. Shay, "Formulary Appointment in the U.S. International Income Tax System: Putting Lipstick on a Pig?," Michigan Journal of International Law, vol. 36, no. 1 (Fall 2014), pp. 1-57.

43 See Michael Durst, "Analysis of a Formulary System, Part VIII: Suggested Statutory, Regulatory Language for Implementing Formulary Apportionment," Tax Management Transfer Pricing Report,, vol. 23, no. 1 (May 1, 2014).

44 U.S. Department of the Treasury, Office of Tax Policy, The Deferral of Income Earned Through U.S. Controlled Foreign Corporations, December 2000, pp. 1-22, http://www.treasury.gov/resource-center/tax-policy/Documents/ subpartf.pdf.

45 The exception has been extended a number of times for various lengths since the most recent version of the provision was enacted by the by the Taxpayer Relief Act of 1997 (P.L. 105-34). The most recent extension was enacted as part of the "extenders package" in P.L. 113-295.

46 Office of Management and Budget, The President's Budget for Fiscal Year 2016, February 2, 2015, https://www.whitehouse.gov/omb/budget, and Office of Management and Budget, The President's Budget for Fiscal Year 2015, March 4, 2014, https://www.whitehouse.gov/omb/budget,

47 For detailed discussions of the revenue consequences of lowering the corporate rate and for reviews of the literature, see CRS Report RL34229, Corporate Tax Reform: Issues for

Congress, by Jane G. Gravelle; and CRS Report R40623, Tax Havens: International Tax Avoidance and Evasion, by Jane G. Gravelle.

[48] For more information, see CRS Report R41743, International Corporate Tax Rate Comparisons and Policy Implications, by Jane G. Gravelle.

[49] Organisation for Economic Co-operation and Development, OECD Secretary-General Report to the G20 Finance Ministers and Central Bank Governors, Istanbul, Turkey, February 2015, p. 3, http://www.oecd.org/tax/oecd-secretarygeneral-tax-report-g20-finance-ministers- february-2015.pdf.

[50] This list is based on the summaries provided by the OECD found here: http:// www.oecd.org/tax/beps-about.htm and http://www.oecd.org/ctp/beps-frequently askedquestions.htm.

[51] In its BEPS FAQ, it includes the following question and response: "48. Are BEPS strategies illegal? Although some schemes used are illegal, most are not. Largely they just take advantage of current rules that are still grounded in a bricks and mortar economic environment rather than today's environment of global players which is characterized by the increasing importance of intangibles and risk management." OECD, OECD/G20 Base Erosion and Profit Shifting Project: Frequently Asked Questions, undated, http://www. oecd.org/ctp/beps-frequently-asked-questions.pdf.

[52] "Pascal Saint-Amans, OECD Tax Policy Head, On Global Tax System Reform, YouTube video, posted by "INSEAD," August 19, 2013, https://www.youtube. com/watch?v =c4effB4i4jk&feature=youtu.be

[53] See question 50 in, OECD, OECD/G20 Base Erosion and Profit Shifting Project: Frequently Asked Questions, undated, http://www.oecd.org/ctp/beps-frequently-asked-questions.pdf.

[54] For a list of current treaties see, Internal Revenue Service, United States Income Tax Treaties—A to Z, http://www.irs.gov/Businesses/International-Businesses/United-States-Income-Tax-Treaties—A-to-Z.

[55] Clark Chandler, Stephen Blough, and Michael Plowgian, "Why U.S. Multinationals Need to Care About BEPS Even if the U.S. Doesn't Change Anything," Daily Tax Report, September 15, 2014.

[56] See, for example, Amanda Athanasiou, "Jumping the Gate on BEPS Unilateral Actions," Tax Notes International, March 16, 2015, pp. 937-939.

[57] See, for example, Vanessa Houlder, "'Hard core' tax dodgers to face strong crackdown," Financial Times, March 14, 2015, online edition, http://www.ft.com/intl/cms/s/0/c745a21e-c8c9-11e4-8617-00144feab7de.html#axzz3UkUZrR4q.

[58] Both of these issues were raised in Clark Chandler, Stephen Blough, and Michael Plowgian, "Why U.S.

Multinationals Need to Care About BEPS Even if the U.S. Doesn't Change Anything," Daily Tax Report, September 15, 2014.

[59] See, for example, Amanda Athanasiou, "The Cost of BEPS: A Question of Balance," Tax Notes International, January 19, 2015, pp. 195-197.

[60] This list is based on, and includes, the summaries provided by the OECD found here: "About BEPS," Organisation for Economic Co-operation and Development, http://www.oecd. org/tax/beps-about.htm; and "BEPS–Frequently Asked Questions," Organisation for Economic Co-operation and Development, http://www.oecd.org/ctp/bepsfrequently askedquestions.htm.

In: Corporate Profit Shifting
Editor: Dorian L. Peters
ISBN: 978-1-63483-767-5

Chapter 2

TAX HAVENS: INTERNATIONAL TAX AVOIDANCE AND EVASION*

Jane G. Gravelle

SUMMARY

Addressing tax evasion and avoidance through use of tax havens has been the subject of a number of proposals in Congress and by the President. Actions by the Organization for Economic Cooperation and Development (OECD) and the G-20 industrialized nations also have addressed this issue. In the 111th Congress, the HIRE Act (P.L. 111-147) included several anti-evasion provisions, and P.L. 111-226 included foreign tax credit provisions directed at perceived abuses by U.S. multinationals. Numerous legislative proposals to address both individual tax evasion and corporate tax avoidance have been advanced.

Multinational firms can artificially shift profits from high-tax to low-tax jurisdictions using a variety of techniques, such as shifting debt to high-tax jurisdictions. Because tax on the income of foreign subsidiaries (except for certain passive income) is deferred until income is repatriated (paid to the U.S. parent as a dividend), this income can avoid current U.S. taxes, perhaps indefinitely. The taxation of passive income (called Subpart F income) has

* This is an edited, reformatted and augmented version of a Congressional Research Service publication R40623, prepared for Members and Committees of Congress dated January 15, 2015.

been reduced, perhaps significantly, through the use of *hybrid entities* that are treated differently in different jurisdictions. The use of hybrid entities was greatly expanded by a new regulation (termed *check- the-box*) introduced in the late 1990s that had unintended consequences for foreign firms. In addition, earnings from income that is taxed often can be shielded by foreign tax credits on other income. On average, very little tax is paid on the foreign source income of U.S. firms. Ample evidence of a significant amount of profit shifting exists, but the revenue cost estimates vary substantially. Evidence also indicates a significant increase in corporate profit shifting over the past several years. Recent estimates suggest losses that may approach, or even exceed, $100 billion per year.

Individuals can evade taxes on passive income, such as interest, dividends, and capital gains, by not reporting income earned abroad. In addition, because interest paid to foreign recipients is not taxed, individuals can evade taxes on U.S. source income by setting up shell corporations and trusts in foreign haven countries to channel funds into foreign jurisdictions. There is no general third-party reporting of income as is the case for ordinary passive income earned domestically; the Internal Revenue Service (IRS) relies on qualified intermediaries (QIs). In the past, these institutions certified nationality without revealing the beneficial owners. Estimates of the cost of individual evasion have ranged from $40 billion to $70 billion. The Foreign Account Tax Compliance Act (FATCA; included in the HIRE Act, P.L. 111-147) introduced required information reporting by foreign financial intermediaries and withholding of tax if information is not provided. These provisions became effective only recently, and their consequences are not yet known.

Most provisions to address profit shifting by multinational firms would involve changing the tax law: repealing or limiting deferral, limiting the ability of the foreign tax credit to offset income, addressing check-the-box, or even formula apportionment. President Obama's proposals include a proposal to disallow overall deductions and foreign tax credits for deferred income, along with a number of other restrictions. Changes in the law or anti-abuse provisions have also been introduced in broader tax reform proposals. Provisions to address individual evasion include increased information reporting and provisions to increase enforcement, such as shifting the burden of proof to the taxpayer, increased penalties, and increased resources. Individual tax evasion is the main target of the HIRE Act, the proposed Stop Tax Haven Abuse Act, and some other proposals.

INTRODUCTION

The federal government loses both individual and corporate income tax revenue from the shifting of profits and income into low-tax countries. The revenue losses from this tax avoidance and evasion are difficult to estimate, but some have suggested that the annual cost of offshore tax abuses may be around $100 billion per year.[1] International tax avoidance can arise from wealthy individual investors and from large multinational corporations; it can reflect both legal and illegal actions.

Tax avoidance is sometimes used to refer to a legal reduction in taxes, whereas evasion refers to tax reductions that are illegal. Both types are discussed in this report, although the dividing line is not entirely clear. A multinational firm that constructs a factory in a low-tax jurisdiction rather than in the United States to take advantage of low foreign corporate tax rates is engaged in avoidance, whereas a U.S. citizen who sets up a secret bank account in the Caribbean and does not report the interest income is engaged in evasion. There are, however, many activities, particularly by corporations, that are often referred to as avoidance but could be classified as evasion. One example is transfer pricing, where firms charge low prices for sales to low-tax affiliates but pay high prices for purchases from them. If these prices, which are supposed to be at arms-length, are set at an artificial level, then this activity might be viewed by some as evasion, even if such pricing is not overturned in court because evidence to establish pricing is not available.

Most of the international tax reduction of individuals reflects evasion, and this amount has been estimated to range from about $40 billion to about $70 billion a year.[2] This evasion has occurred in part because the United States does not withhold tax on many types of passive income (such as interest) paid to foreign entities; if U.S. individuals can channel their investments through a foreign entity and do not report the holdings of these assets on their tax returns, they evade a tax that they are legally required to pay. In addition, individuals investing in foreign assets may not report income from these assets. In 2010, Congress enacted the Foreign Account Tax Compliance Act (FATCA),[3] which has recently become effective and requires foreign financial institutions to report information on asset holders or be subject to a 30% withholding rate. Its consequences for evasion have yet to be determined.

Corporate tax reductions arising from profit shifting also have been estimated. As discussed below, estimates of the revenue losses from corporate profit shifting vary substantially, ranging from about $10 billion to about $90 billion, or even higher.[4] This activity appears to have increased substantially in recent years.

In addition to differentiating between individual and corporate activities, and evasion and avoidance, there are also variations in the features used to characterize tax havens. Some restrictive definitions would limit tax havens to those countries that, in addition to having low or non-existent tax rates on some types of income, also have such other characteristics as the lack of transparency, bank secrecy and the lack of information sharing, and requiring little or no economic activity for an entity to obtain legal status. A definition incorporating compounding factors such as these was used by the Organization for Economic Development and Cooperation (OECD) in their 2000 tax shelter initiative. Others, particularly economists, might characterize as a tax haven any low-tax country with a goal of attracting capital, or simply any country that has low or non-existent taxes. This report addresses tax havens in their broader sense as well as in their narrower sense.

Although international tax avoidance can be differentiated by whether it is associated with individuals or corporations, whether it is illegal evasion or legal avoidance, and whether it arises in a tax haven narrowly defined or broadly defined, it can also be characterized by what measures might be taken to reduce this loss. In general, revenue losses from individual taxes are more likely to be associated with evasion and more likely to be associated with narrowly defined tax havens, while corporate tax avoidance occurs in both narrowly and broadly defined tax havens and can arise from either legal avoidance or illegal evasion. Evasion is often a problem of lack of information, and remedies may include resources for enforcement, along with incentives and sanctions designed to increase information sharing, and possibly a move towards greater withholding. Avoidance may be more likely to be remedied with changes in the tax code.

Several legislative proposals have been advanced that address international tax issues. President Obama has proposed several international corporate tax revisions which relate to multinational corporations, including profit shifting, as well as individual tax evasion. Some of the provisions relating to multinationals had earlier been included in a bill introduced in the 110th Congress by Chairman Rangel of the Ways and Means Committee (H.R. 3970). Major revisions to corporate international tax rules were also included in S. 3018, a general tax reform act introduced by Senators Wyden and Gregg in the 111th Congress, and a similar bill, S. 727, introduced by Senators Wyden and Coats in the 112th Congress.[5] This bill had provisions to tax foreign source income currently, which could have limited the benefits from corporate profit shifting. In the 113th Congress, H.R. 694 (Representative Schakowsky) and S. 250 (Senator Sanders), also would have eliminated deferral. Former Ways and Means Chairman Dave Camp has proposed a lower corporate rate combined with a move to a territorial tax system (which would exempt foreign source income). His bill, H.R. 1 (a general tax reform bill), was introduced in the 113th Congress. Because a territorial tax could increase the scope for profit shifting, the proposal contains detailed provisions to address these issues. A territorial tax proposal with anti-abuse provisions has also been introduced by Senator Enzi (S. 2091, 112th Congress).[6]

The Senate Permanent Subcommittee on Investigations has been engaged in international tax investigations since 2001, holding hearings and proposing legislation.[7] In the 111th Congress, the Stop Tax Haven Abuse Act, S. 506, was introduced by the chairman of that committee, Senator Levin, with a companion bill, H.R. 1265, introduced by Representative Doggett. The Senate Finance Committee also has circulated draft proposals addressing individual tax evasion issues. A number of these anti-evasion provisions (including provisions in President Obama's earlier budget outlines) were adopted in the Hiring Incentives to Restore Employment (HIRE) Act, P.L. 111-147. Subsequently, revised versions of the Stop Tax Haven Abuse Act have been introduced.[8] The Permanent Subcommittee also released a study of profit shifting by multinationals in preparation for a hearing on September 20, 2012.[9]

The first section of this report reviews what countries might be considered tax havens, including a discussion of the Organization for Economic Development and Cooperation (OECD) initiatives and lists. The next two sections discuss, in turn, the corporate profit-shifting mechanisms and evidence on the existence and magnitude of profit-shifting activity. The following two sections provide the same analysis for individual tax evasion. The report concludes with overviews of alternative policy options, a summary of legislation enacted in the 111th Congress, and a summary of specific legislative proposals.

WHERE ARE THE TAX HAVENS?

There is no precise definition of a tax haven. The OECD initially defined the following features of tax havens: no or low taxes, lack of effective exchange of information, lack of transparency, and no requirement of substantial activity.[10] Other lists have been developed in legislative proposals and by researchers. Also, a number of other jurisdictions have been identified as having tax haven characteristics.

Formal Lists of Tax Havens

The OECD created an initial list of tax havens in 2000. A similar list was used in S. 396, introduced in the 110th Congress, which would have treated firms incorporated in certain tax havens as domestic companies; the only difference between this list and the OECD list was the exclusion of the U.S. Virgin Islands from the list in S. 396. Legislation introduced in the 111th Congress to address tax haven abuse (S. 506, H.R. 1265) used a different list taken from Internal Revenue Service (IRS) court filings but had many countries in common. The definition by the OECD excluded low-tax jurisdictions, some of which are OECD members that were thought by many to be tax havens, such as Ireland and Switzerland. These countries were included in an important study of tax havens by Hines and Rice.[11] The Government Accountability Office (GAO) also provided a list.[12]

Table 1 lists the countries that appear on various lists, arranged by geographic location. These tax havens tend to be concentrated in certain areas, including the Caribbean and West Indies and Europe, locations close to large developed countries. There are 50 altogether.

Table 1. Countries Listed on Various Tax Haven Lists

Caribbean/West Indies	Anguilla, Antigua and Barbuda, Aruba, Bahamas, Barbados,[e,e] British Virgin Islands, Cayman Islands, Dominica, Grenada, Montserrat,a Netherlands Antilles, St. Kitts and Nevis, St. Lucia, St. Vincent and Grenadines, Turks and Caicos, U.S. Virgin Islands[a,e]
Central America	Belize, Costa Rica,[b,c] Panama
Coast of East Asia	Hong Kong,[b,e] Macau,[a,b,e] Singaporeb
Europe/Mediterranean	Andorra,[a] Channel Islands (Guernsey and Jersey),[e] Cyprus,[e] Gibralter, Isle of Man,[e] Ireland,[a,b,e] Liechtenstein, Luxembourg,[a,b,e] Malta,[e] Monaco,[a] San Marino,[a,e] Switzerland[a,b]
Indian Ocean	Maldives,[a,d] Mauritius,[a,c,e] Seychellesa,[e]
Middle East	Bahrain, Jordan,[a,b] Lebanona,[b]
North Atlantic	Bermudae

Pacific, South Pacific	Cook Islands, Marshall Islands,[a] Samoa, Nauru,c Niue,[a,c] Tonga,[a,c,d] Vanuatu
West Africa	Liberia

Sources: Organization for Economic Development and Cooperation (OECD), Towards Global Tax Competition, 2000; Dhammika Dharmapala and James R. Hines, "Which Countries Become Tax Havens?" Journal of Public Economics, Vol. 93, 0ctober 2009, pp. 1058-1068; Tax Justice Network, "Identifying Tax Havens and Offshore Finance Centers: http://www.taxjustice.net/cms/upload/pdf/Identifying_Tax_Havens_Jul_07.pdf. The OECD's gray list is posted at http://www.oecd.org/dataoecd/38/14/42497950.pdf. The countries in Table 1 are the same as the countries, with the exception of Tonga, in a 2008 Government Accountability Office (GAO) Report, *International Taxation: Large U.S. Corporations and Federal Contractors with Subsidiaries in Jurisdictions Listed as Tax Havens or Financial Privacy Jurisdictions*, GAO-09-157, December 2008.

Notes: The Dharmapala and Hines paper cited above reproduces the Hines and Rice list. That list was more oriented to business issues; four countries—Ireland, Jordan, Luxembourg, and Switzerland—appear only on that list. The Hines and Rice list is older and is itself based on earlier lists; some countries on those earlier lists were eliminated because they had higher tax rates.

In 2010, the Netherlands Antilles dissolved, with the islands of Curacao and St. Maarten becoming autonomous and the islands of Belaire, St. Eustastius, and Saba becoming part of the Netherlands. Curacao has indicated a plan to phase out its favorable tax treatment of offshore firms.

St. Kitts may also be referred to as St. Christopher. The Channel Islands are sometimes listed as a group, and sometimes Jersey and Guernsey are listed separately. S. 506 and H.R. 1245 specifically mention Jersey and also refer to Gurensey/Sark/Alderney; the latter two are islands associated with Guernsey.

a. Not included in S. 506, H.R. 1245.

b. Not included in original OECD tax haven list.

c. Not included in Hines and Rice (1994).

d. Removed from OECD's list; subsequently determined they should not be included.

e. Not included in OECD's gray list as of August 17, 2009; currently on the OECD white list. Note that the gray list is divided into countries that are tax havens and countries that are other financial centers. The latter classification includes three countries listed in Table 1 (Luxembourg, Singapore, and Switzerland) and five that are not (Austria, Belgium, Brunei, Chile, and Guatemala). Of the four countries moved from the black to the gray list, one, Costa Rica, is in **Table 1** and three, Malaysia, Uruguay, and the Philippines, are not.

Developments in the OECD Tax Haven List

The OECD list, the most prominent list, has changed over time. Nine of the countries in **Table 1** did not appear on the earliest OECD list. These countries not appearing on the original list tend to be more developed larger countries and include some that are members of the OECD (e.g., Switzerland and Luxembourg).

It is also important to distinguish between OECD's original list and its blacklist. OECD subsequently focused on information exchange and removed countries from a blacklist if they agree to cooperate. OECD initially examined 47 jurisdictions and identified a number as not meeting the criteria for a tax haven; it also initially excluded six countries with advance agreements to share information (Bermuda, the Cayman Islands, Cyprus, Malta, Mauritius, and San Marino). The 2000 OECD blacklist included 35 countries; this list did not include the six countries eliminated due to advance agreement. The OECD had also subsequently determined that three countries should not be included in the list of tax havens (Barbados, the Maldives, and Tonga). Over time, as more tax havens made agreements to share information, the blacklist dwindled until it included only three countries: Andorra, Liechtenstein, and Monaco.

A study of the OECD initiative on global tax coordination by Sharman, also discussed in a book review by Sullivan, argues that the reduction in the OECD list was not because of actual progress towards cooperation so much as due to the withdrawal of U.S. support in 2001, which resulted in the OECD focusing on information on request and not requiring reforms until all parties had signed on.[13] This analysis suggests that the large countries were not successful in this initiative to rein in on tax havens. A similar analysis by Spencer and Sharman suggests little real progress has been made in reducing tax haven practices.[14]

Interest in tax haven actions has increased recently. The scandals surrounding the Swiss bank UBS AG (UBS) and the Liechtenstein Global Trust Group (LGT), which led to legal actions by the United States and other countries, focused greater attention on international tax issues, primarily information reporting and individual evasion.[15] The credit crunch and provision of public funds to banks has also heightened public interest. The tax haven issue was revived recently with a meeting of the G20 industrialized and developing countries that proposed sanctions, and a number of countries began to indicate commitments to information sharing agreements.[16]

The OECD currently has three lists: a *white list* of countries implementing an agreed-upon standard, a *gray list* of countries that have committed to such a standard, and a *black list* of countries that have not committed. On April 7, 2009, the last four countries on the black list, which were countries not included on the original OECD list—Costa Rica, Malaysia, the Philippines, and Uruguay—were moved to the gray list.[17] The gray list includes countries not identified as tax havens but as "other financial centers." According to news reports, Hong Kong and Macau were omitted from the OECD's list because of objections from China, but are mentioned in a footnote as having committed to the standards; they also noted that a "recent flurry of commitments brought 11 jurisdictions, including Austria, Liechtenstein, Luxembourg, Singapore, and Switzerland into the committed category."[18] As of May 18, 2012, only one country (Nauru) appeared on the gray list for tax havens and one (Guatemala) appeared on the gray list for financial centers.[19]

Many countries that were listed on the OECD's original blacklist protested because of the negative publicity and many now point to having signed agreements to negotiate tax information exchange agreements (TIEA) and some have negotiated agreements. The identification of tax havens can have legal ramifications if laws and sanctions are contingent on that identification, as is the case of some current proposals in the United States and of potential sanctions by international bodies.

More recently, the OECD has focused attention on its Base Erosion and Profit Shifting (BEPS) initiative. Among the elements of this initiative is the Global Forum on Transparency and Exchange of Information for Tax Purposes, which has begun rating countries on various criteria. As of October 2014, it had under way 105 reviews of countries based on various standards.[20] The countries are rated as compliant, largely compliant, partially compliant, or noncompliant. As of 2014, 71 jurisdictions had received a full review, with 42 of those rated as noncompliant. Of 34 countries that had undergone only a phase 1 review, which examines the legal and regulatory framework, 12 were not able to advance to the final (phase 2) review, which looks into the implementation of the regulatory framework in practice. As with the evolution of the OECD list, these evaluations focus on one aspect of the characteristics of tax havens.

Other Jurisdictions with Tax Haven Characteristics

Criticisms have been made by a range of commentators that many countries are tax havens or have aspects of tax havens and have been overlooked. These jurisdictions include major countries such as the United

States, the UK, the Netherlands, Denmark, Hungary, Iceland, Israel, Portugal, and Canada. Attention has also been directed at three states in the United States: Delaware, Nevada, and Wyoming. Finally, there are a number of smaller countries or areas in countries, such as Campione d'Italia, an Italian town located within Switzerland, that have been characterized as tax havens.

A country not on the list in **Table 1**, but which is often considered a tax haven, especially for corporations, is the Netherlands, which allows firms to reduce taxes on dividends and capital gains from subsidiaries and has a wide range of treaties that reduce taxes.[21] In 2006, for example, Bono and other members of the U2 band moved their music publishing company from Ireland to the Netherlands after Ireland changed its tax treatment of music royalties.[22] A 2010 newspaper report explained the role of the Netherlands in facilitating movement to tax havens through provisions such as the various "Dutch sandwiches," which allow money to be funneled out of other countries that would charge withholding taxes to non-European countries, to be passed on in turn to tax havens such as Bermuda and the Cayman Islands.[23] Issues have recently been raised in the Netherlands government about its role in tax avoidance.[24] The European Commission also began investigating, in June 2014, whether certain arrangements in Ireland, Luxembourg, and the Netherlands constitute prohibited state aid; the inquiry was later expanded to all member states.[25] In addition, the European Union has agreed to add an anti-abuse clause to its provision to prevent double taxation within member states, which may have implications for these arrangements in the future.[26]

Some have identified the United States and the United Kingdom (UK) as having tax haven characteristics. Luxembourg Prime Minister Jean-Claude Junker urged other EU member states to challenge the United States for tax havens in Delaware, Nevada, and Wyoming.[27] One website offering offshore services mentions, in their view, several overlooked tax havens which include the United States, United Kingdom, Denmark, Iceland, Israel, and Portugal's Madeira Island.[28] (Others on their list and not listed in **Table 1** were Hungary, Brunei, Uruguay, and Labuan [Malaysia]).[29] In the case of the United States the article mentions the lack of reporting requirements and the failure to tax interest and other exempt passive income paid to foreign entities, the limited liability corporation which allows a flexible corporate vehicle not subject to taxation, and the ease of incorporating in certain states (Delaware, Nevada, and Wyoming). Issues have recently been raised in the Netherlands about its role in tax avoidance

Another website includes in its list of tax havens Delaware, Wyoming, and Puerto Rico, along with other jurisdictions not listed in **Table 1:** the

Netherlands, Campione d'Italia, a separate listing for Sark (identified as the only remaining "fiscal paradise"), the UK, and a coming discussion for Canada.[30] Sark is an island country associated with Guernsey, part of the Channel Islands, and Campione d'Italia is an Italian town located within Switzerland.

The Economist reported a study by a political scientist experimenting with setting up sham corporations; the author succeeded in incorporating in Wyoming and Nevada, as well as the UK and several other places.[31] Michael McIntyre discusses three U.S. practices that aid international evasion: the failure to collect information on tax exempt interest income paid to foreign entities, the system of foreign institutions that act as qualified intermediaries (see discussion below) but do not reveal their clients, and the practices of states such as Delaware and Wyoming that allow people to keep secret their identities as stockholder or depositor.[32]

In a meeting in late April 2009, Eduardo Silva, of the Cayman Islands Financial Services Association, claimed that Delaware, Nevada, Wyoming, and the UK were the greatest offenders with respect to, among other issues, tax fraud. He suggested that Nevada and Wyoming were worse than Delaware because they permit companies to have bearer shares, which allows anonymous ownership. A U.S. participant at the conference noted that legislation in the United States, S. 569 (111th Congress), would require disclosure of beneficial owners in the United States.[33]

Nicholas Shaxson, in his book *Treasure Islands*, organizes tax havens into four categories: (1) continental European havens such as Switzerland and Luxembourg; (2) a British zone of influence (which includes the City of London[34] as well as countries formally related to the UK, such as Jersey, Guernsey, the Isle of Man, Bermuda, and many of the islands in the West Indies and Caribbean, and those influenced by the UK); (3) a U.S. zone of influence (the United States itself, some of its states, along with the Virgin Islands, Marshall Islands, Liberia, and Panama), and (4) other jurisdictions.[35] Anthony van Fossen, in his study of Pacific Island tax havens, indicates that connection with the UK and specifically with the City of London is a contributor to a successful tax haven. While the United States has limited the activities of some islands in its sphere of influence, one of the most important tax havens in this area is the Marshall Islands, which specializes in flags of convenience.[36]

In addition, any country with a low tax rate could be considered as a potential location for shifting income to. In addition to Ireland, three other countries in the OECD not included in **Table 1** have tax rates below 20%:

Iceland, Poland, and the Slovak Republic.[37] Most of the eastern European countries not included in the OECD have tax rates below 20%.[38]

The Tax Justice Network probably has the largest list of tax havens, and includes some specific cities and areas.[39] In addition to the countries listed in **Table 1**, they include in the Americas and Caribbean, New York and Uruguay; in Africa, Mellila, Sao Tome e Principe, Somalia, and South Africa; in the Middle East and Asia, Dubai, Labuan (Malaysia), Tel Aviv, and Taipei; in Europe, Alderney, Belgium, Campione d'Italia, City of London, Dublin, Ingushetia, Madeira, Sark, Trieste, Turkish Republic of Northern Cyprus, and Frankfurt; and in the Indian and Pacific oceans, the Marianas. The only county listed in **Table 1** and not included in their list was Jordan.

Ronen Palan, Richard Murphy, and Christian Chavagneux report 11 different lists of tax havens. Although the Tax Justice Network is the largest such list, a few countries not on this list appear on others.[40] Eight countries appeared on all lists: the Bahamas, Bermuda, the Cayman Islands, Guernsey, Jersey, and Malta. Palan, Murphy, and Chavagneux also suggest adding Belgium to the Netherlands and Luxembourg as a location for holding companies in Europe. In addition, they discuss the aspects of rules in the United States and the United Kingdom that might justify identification as a tax haven.

METHODS OF CORPORATE TAX AVOIDANCE

U.S. multinationals are not taxed on income earned by foreign subsidiaries until it is repatriated to the U.S. parent as dividends, although some passive and related company income that is easily shifted is taxed currently under anti-abuse rules referred to as Subpart F. (Foreign affiliates or subsidiaries that are majority owned U.S. owned are referred to as controlled foreign corporations, or CFCs, and many of these related firms are wholly owned.) Taxes on income that is repatriated (or, less commonly, earned by branches and taxed currently) are allowed a credit for foreign income taxes paid. (A part of a parent company treated as a branch is not a separate entity for tax purposes, and all income is part of the parent's income.)

Foreign tax credits are limited to the amount of tax imposed by the United States, so that they, in theory, cannot offset taxes on domestic income. This limit is imposed on an overall basis, allowing excess credits in high-tax countries to offset U.S. tax liability on income earned in low- tax countries, although separate limits apply to passive and active income. Other countries either employ this system of deferral and credit or, more commonly, exempt income earned in foreign jurisdictions. Most countries have some form of anti-abuse rules similar to Subpart F.

If a firm can shift profits to a low-tax jurisdiction from a high-tax one, its taxes will be reduced without affecting other aspects of the company. Tax differences also affect real economic activity, which in turn affects revenues, but it is this artificial shifting of profits that is the focus of this report.[41]

Because the United States taxes all income earned in its borders as well as imposing a residual tax on income earned abroad by U.S. persons, tax avoidance relates both to U.S. parent companies shifting profits abroad to low-tax jurisdictions and the shifting of profits out of the United States by foreign parents of U.S. subsidiaries. In the case of U.S. multinationals, one study suggested that about half the difference between profitability in low-tax and high-tax countries, which could arise from artificial income shifting, was due to transfers of intellectual property (or intangibles) and most of the rest through the allocation of debt.[42] However, a study examining import and export prices suggests a very large effect of transfer pricing in goods (as discussed below).[43] Some evidence of the importance of intellectual property can also be found from the types of firms that repatriated profits abroad following a temporary tax reduction enacted in 2004; one- third of the repatriations were in the pharmaceutical and medicine industry and almost 20% in the computer and electronic equipment industry.[44]

Allocation of Debt and Earnings Stripping

One method of shifting profits from a high-tax jurisdiction to a low-tax one is to borrow more in the high-tax jurisdiction and less in the low-tax one. This shifting of debt can be achieved without changing the overall debt exposure of the firm. A more specific practice is referred to as earnings stripping, where either debt is associated with related firms or unrelated debt is not subject to tax by the recipient. As an example of the former earnings stripping method, a foreign parent may lend to its U.S. subsidiary. Alternatively, an unrelated foreign borrower not subject to tax on U.S. interest income might lend to a U.S. firm.

The U.S. tax code currently contains provisions to address interest deductions and earnings stripping. It applies an allocation of the U.S. parent's interest for purposes of the limit on the foreign tax credit. The amount of foreign source income is reduced when part of U.S. interest is allocated and the maximum amount of foreign tax credits taken is limited, a provision that affects firms with excess foreign tax credits.[45] There is no allocation rule, however, to address deferral, so that a U.S. parent could operate its subsidiary with all equity finance in a low-tax jurisdiction and take all of the interest on the overall firm's debt as a deduction. A bill introduced in 2007 (H.R. 3970) by Chairman Rangel of the Ways and Means Committee would introduce such an allocation rule, so that a portion of interest and other overhead costs would not be deducted until the income is repatriated.[46] This provision is also included in President Obama's proposals for international tax revision and in some congressional proposals.

While allocation-of-interest approaches could be used to address allocation of interest to high-tax countries in the case of U.S. multinationals, they cannot be applied to U.S. subsidiaries of foreign corporations. To limit the scope of earnings stripping in either case, the United States has thin capitalization rules. (Most of the United States' major trading partners have similar rules.) A section of the Internal Revenue Code (163(j)) applies to a corporation with a debt-to-equity ratio above 1.5 to 1 and with net interest exceeding 50% of adjusted taxable income (generally taxable income plus interest plus depreciation). Interest in excess of the 50% limit paid to a related corporation is not deductible if the corporation is not subject to U.S. income tax. This interest restriction also applies to interest paid to unrelated parties that are not taxed to the recipient.

The possibility of earnings stripping received more attention after a number of U.S. firms inverted, that is, arranged to move their parent firm abroad so that U.S. operations became a subsidiary of that parent. The American Jobs Creation Act of 2004 (AJCA; P.L. 108-357) addressed the general problem of inversion by treating firms that subsequently inverted as U.S. firms. During consideration of this legislation there were also proposals for broader earnings stripping restrictions as an approach to this problem that would have reduced the excess interest deductions. This general earnings stripping proposal was not adopted. However, the AJCA mandated a Treasury Department study on this and other issues; that study focused on U.S. subsidiaries of foreign parents and was not able to find clear evidence on the magnitude.[47]

Noted in the Treasury's mandated study, there is relatively straightforward evidence that U.S. multinationals allocate more interest to high-tax jurisdictions, but it is more difficult to assess earnings stripping by foreign parents of U.S. subsidiaries, because the entire firm's accounts are not available. The Treasury study focused on this issue and used an approach that had been used in the past of comparing these subsidiaries to U.S. firms. The study was not able to provide conclusive evidence about the shifting of profits out of the United States due to high leverage rates for U.S. subsidiaries of foreign firms but did find evidence of shifting for inverted firms.

Inversions have recently become an issue. Although some firms inverted following the 2004 legislation based on an activity exception, that approach was limited by regulation. In 2014, a number of U.S. firms inverted, or considered inversion, by merging with a smaller foreign firm. The President has proposed tighter restrictions on these inversions, and two bills regarding this matter, H.R. 4679 and S. 2360, were introduced in the 113th Congress. Regulatory changes to limit some of the benefits have been made.[48]

Transfer Pricing

The second major way that firms can shift profits from high-tax to low-tax jurisdictions is through the pricing of goods and services sold between affiliates. To properly reflect income, prices of goods and services sold by related companies should be the same as the prices that would be paid by unrelated parties. By lowering the price of goods and services sold by parents and affiliates in high-tax jurisdictions and raising the price of purchases, income can be shifted.

An important and growing issue of transfer pricing is with the transfers to rights to intellectual property, or intangibles. If a patent developed in the United States is licensed to an affiliate in a low-tax country income will be shifted if the royalty or other payment is lower than the true value of the license. For many goods there are similar products sold or other methods (such as cost plus a markup) that can be used to determine whether prices are set appropriately. Intangibles, such as new inventions or new drugs, tend not to have comparables, and it is very difficult to know the royalty that would be paid in an arms-length price. Therefore, intangibles represent particular problems for policing transfer pricing.

Investment in intangibles is favorably treated in the United States because costs, other than capital equipment and buildings, are expensed for research and development, which is also eligible for a tax credit. In addition, advertising to establish brand names is also deductible. Overall these treatments tend to produce an effective low, zero, or negative tax rate for overall investment in intangibles. Thus, there are significant incentives to make these investments in the United States. On average, the benefit of tax deductions or credits when making the investment tend to offset the future taxes on the return to the investment. However, for those investments that tend to be successful, it is advantageous to shift profits to a low-tax jurisdiction, so that there are tax savings on investment and little or no tax on returns. As a result, these investments can be subject to negative tax rates, or subsidies, which can be significant.

Transfer pricing rules with respect to intellectual property are further complicated because of cost sharing agreements, where different affiliates contribute to the cost.[49] If an intangible is already partially developed by the parent firm, affiliates contribute a buy-in payment. It is very difficult to determine arms-length pricing in these cases where a technology is partially developed and there is risk associated with the expected outcome. One study found some evidence that firms with cost sharing arrangements were more likely to engage in profit shifting.[50]

One problem with shifting profits to some tax haven jurisdictions is that, if real activity is necessary to produce the intangible these countries may not have labor and other resources to undertake the activity. However, firms have developed techniques to take advantage of tax laws in other countries to achieve both a productive operation while shifting profits to no-tax jurisdictions. An example is the *double Irish, Dutch sandwich* method that has been used by some U.S. firms, including, as exposed in news articles, Google.[51] In this arrangement, the U.S. firm transfers its intangible asset to an Irish holding company. This company has a subsidiary sales company that sells advertising (the source of Google's revenues) to Europe. However, sandwiched between the Irish holding company and the Irish sales subsidiary is a Dutch subsidiary, which collects royalties from the sales subsidiary and transfers them to the Irish holding company. The Irish holding company claims company management (and tax home) in Bermuda, with a 0% tax rate, for purposes of the corporate income tax. This strategy allows the Irish operation to avoid even the low Irish tax of 12.5% and, by using the Dutch sandwich, to avoid Irish withholding taxes (which are not due on payments to European Union companies). More recently, European countries have complained about companies such as Google, Apple, Amazon, Facebook, and Starbucks using this strategy in some cases.

Ireland has indicated it will be ending the rule that allows a firm to be incorporated in Ireland but have its tax home elsewhere, although the country will retain its low 12.5% corporate tax rate and is considering a lower rate for earnings from technology.[52] Profits can also be shifted directly to a tax haven, as in the case of Yahoo, where the Dutch intermediary can transfer profits directly to the tax haven (in this case, the Cayman islands) because it does not collect a withholding tax, as would be the case with France or Ireland.[53]

Contract Manufacturing

When a subsidiary is set up in a low-tax country and profit shifting occurs, as in the acquisition of rights to an intangible, a further problem occurs: this low-tax country may not be a desirable place to actually manufacture and sell the product. For example, an Irish subsidiary's market may be in Germany and it would be desirable to manufacture in Germany. But to earn profits in Germany with its higher tax rate does not minimize taxes. Instead the Irish firm may contract with a German firm as a contract manufacturer, who will produce the item for cost plus a fixed markup. Subpart F taxes on a current basis certain profits from sales income, so the arrangement must be structured to qualify as an exception from this rule. There are complex and changing regulations on this issue.[54]

Check-the-Box, Hybrid Entities, and Hybrid Instruments

Another technique for shifting profit to low-tax jurisdictions was greatly expanded with the *check-the-box* provisions. These provisions were originally intended to simplify questions of whether a firm was a corporation or a partnership. Their application to foreign circumstances through the disregarded entity rules has led to the expansion of hybrid entities, where an entity can be recognized as a corporation by one jurisdiction but not by another. For example, a U.S. parent's subsidiary in a low-tax country can lend to its subsidiary in a high-tax country, with the interest deductible because the high-tax country recognizes the firm as a separate corporation. Normally, interest received by the subsidiary in the low-tax country would be considered passive or *tainted* income subject to current U.S. tax under Subpart F. However, under check-the-box rules, the high-tax corporation can elect to be disregarded as a separate entity. Thus, from the perspective of the United States, there would be no interest income paid because the two are the same entity. Check-the-box and similar hybrid entity operations also can be used to avoid other types of Subpart F income, for example from contract manufacturing arrangements. According to David R. Sicular, this provision, which began as a regulation, has been, albeit temporarily, codified (called the *look-through rules*).[55] The look-through rules expand the scope of check-the-box to more related parties and circumstances. They began as temporary provisions but have been extended numerous times. Currently, they expired at the end of 2014.

Hybrid entities relate to issues other than Subpart F. For example, a reverse hybrid entity formerly could be used to allow U.S. corporations to benefit from the foreign tax credit without having to recognize the underlying income. As an example, a U.S. parent could have set up a holding company in a county that was treated as a disregarded entity, and the holding company could have owned a corporation that was treated as a partnership in another foreign jurisdiction. Under flow-through rules, the holding company was liable for the foreign tax and, because it was not a separate entity, the U.S. parent corporation was therefore liable, but the income could have been retained in the foreign corporation that was viewed as a separate corporate entity from the U.S. point of view. In this case, the entity was structured so that it was a partnership for foreign purposes but a corporation for U.S. purposes.[56] Provisions in P.L. 111-226 eliminated this practice.

In addition to hybrid entities that achieve tax benefits by being treated differently in the United States and the foreign jurisdiction, there are also hybrid instruments that can avoid taxation by being treated as debt in one jurisdiction and equity in another.[57]

Cross Crediting and Sourcing Rules for Foreign Tax Credits

Income from a low-tax country that is received in the United States can escape taxes because of cross crediting: the use of excess foreign taxes paid in one jurisdiction or on one type of income to offset U.S. tax that would be due on other income. In some periods in the past the foreign tax credit limit was proposed on a country-by-country basis, although that rule proved to be difficult to enforce given the potential to use holding companies. Foreign tax credits have subsequently been separated into different baskets to limit cross crediting; these baskets were reduced from nine to two (active and passive) in the American Jobs Creation Act of 2004.

Because firms can choose when to repatriate income, they can arrange realizations to maximize the benefits of the overall limit on the foreign tax credit. That is, firms that have income from jurisdictions with taxes in excess of U.S. taxes can also elect to realize income from jurisdictions with low taxes and use the excess credits to offset U.S. tax due on that income. Studies suggest that between cross crediting and deferral, U.S. multinationals typically pay virtually no U.S. tax on foreign source income.[58]

This ability to reduce U.S. tax due to cross crediting is increased, it can be argued, because income that should be considered U.S. source income is treated as foreign source income, thereby raising the foreign tax credit limit. This includes income from U.S. exports which is U.S. source income, because a tax provision (referred to as the title passage rule) allows half of export income to be allocated to the country in which the title passes. Another important type of income that is considered foreign source and thus can be shielded with foreign tax credits is royalty income from active business, which has become an increasingly important source of foreign income. This benefit can occur in high-tax countries because royalties are generally deductible from income. (Note that the shifting of income due to transfer pricing of intangibles, advantageous in low-tax countries, is a different issue.) Interest income is another type of income that may benefit from this foreign tax credit rule.

Since all of this income arises from investment in the United States, one could argue that this income is appropriately U.S. source income, or that, failing that, it should be put in a different foreign tax credit basket so that excess credits generated by dividends cannot be used to offset such income. Two studies, by Harry Grubert and by Grubert and Rosanne Altshuler, have discussed this sourcing rule in the context of a proposal to eliminate the tax on active dividends.[59] In that proposal, the revenue loss from exempting active dividends from U.S. tax would be offset by gains from taxes on royalties.

In addition to these general policy issues, there are numerous other, narrower techniques that might be used to enhance foreign tax credits; several of these were the focus of legislation in H.R. 4213, the American Jobs and Loophole Closing Act, with most provisions enacted in P.L. 111- 226.

THE MAGNITUDE OF CORPORATE PROFIT SHIFTING

This section examines the evidence on the existence and magnitude of profit shifting and the techniques that are most likely to contribute to it.

Evidence on the Scope of Profit Shifting

There is ample, and simple, evidence that profits appear in countries inconsistent with an economic motivation. This section first examines the profit share of income of controlled corporations compared to the share of gross domestic product and how it has changed recently.[60]

The first set of countries, acting as a reference point, includes the remaining G-7 countries that are also among the United States' major trading partners. These countries account for 12% of pretax profits and 21% of rest-of-world gross domestic product. The second group of countries includes larger countries from **Table 1** (with gross domestic product [GDP] of at least $15 billion), plus the Netherlands, which is widely considered a tax conduit for U.S. multinationals because of its holding company rules. These countries account for about 40% of earnings and 4% of rest-of-world GDP. The third group of countries includes smaller countries listed in **Table 1**, with GDP less than $10 billion. These countries account for 18% of earnings and less than one- tenth of 1% of rest-of-world GDP.[61]

As indicated in **Table 2**, income-to-GDP ratios in the large G-7 countries in 2010 ranged from 0.2% to 3.3%, the larger amounts reflecting in part the United States' relationships with some of its closest trading partners. Overall, this income as a share of GDP is 0.7%. Outside the UK and Canada, this income as a share of GDP is around 0.3% to 0.6% and does not vary with country size (Japan, for example, has over twice the GDP of Italy). Canada and the UK also have appeared on some tax haven lists, and the larger income shares could partially reflect that fact.[62] There has been relatively little change in the aggregate between 2004 and 2010 (the latest year IRS data on earnings of multinational firms are available).

Table 2. U.S. Company Foreign Profits Relative to Gross Domestic Product (GDP), G-7

Country	Profits of U.S. Controlled Foreign Corporations as a Percentage of GDP, 2004	Profits of U.S. Controlled Foreign Corporations as a Percentage of GDP, 2010
Canada	2.6	3.3
France	0.3	0.6
Germany	0.2	0.4
Italy	0.2	0.3
Japan	0.3	0.4
United Kingdom	1.3	2.1
Weighted Average	0.6	0.7

Source: Congressional Research Service (CRS) calculations, see text.

Table 3. U.S. Foreign Company Profits Relative to GDP, Larger Countries (GDP at Least $15 billion) on Tax Haven Lists and the Netherlands

Country	Profits of U.S. Controlled Corporations as a Percentage of GDP, 2004	Profits of U.S. Controlled Corporations as a Percentage of GDP, 2010
Costa Rica	1.2	—
Cyprus	9.8	13.6
Hong Kong	2.8	2.6
Ireland	7.6	41.9
Luxembourg	18.2	127.0
Netherlands	4.6	17.1
Panama	3.0	0.1
Singapore	3.4	4.7
Switzerland	3.5	12.3

Source: CRS calculations, see text.

Note: Dashes indicate data not available. Profits data for Costa Rica, which were listed separately in the 2008 tax data indicate a 1.2% share.

Table 3 reports the share for the larger tax havens listed in **Table 1** for which data are available, plus the Netherlands. In general, U.S. source profits as a percentage of GDP are considerably larger than those in **Table 2**. In the case of Luxembourg, these profits were 18% of output in 2004 and 127% in 2010. Shares are also very large in Ireland and the Netherlands (42% and 17%, respectively), where they have both grown substantially. Shares in Switzerland and Cyprus have also grown. In most cases, the shares are well in excess of those in **Table 2**.

Table 4 examines the small tax havens listed in **Table 1** for which data are available. In Bermuda, the British Virgin Islands, and the Cayman Islands profits are multiples of total GDP and in all cases have grown substantially. Profits are well in excess of GDP in four jurisdictions for 2004 (the three above plus the Marshall Islands), although data for the Marshall Islands are not available for 2010. In other jurisdictions in **Table 4**, profits are a large share of output. These numbers clearly indicate that the profits in these countries do not appear to derive from economic motives related to productive inputs or markets but rather reflect income easily transferred to low- tax jurisdictions.

Table 4. U.S. Foreign Company Profits Relative to GDP, Small Countries on Tax Haven Lists

Country	Profits of U.S. Controlled Corporations as a Percentage of GDP, 2004	Profits of U.S. Controlled Corporations as a Percentage of GDP, 2010
Bahamas	43.3	70.8
Barbados	13.2	5.7
Bermuda	645.7	1614.0
British Virgin Islands	354.7	1803.7
Cayman Islands	546.7	2065.5
Guernsey	11.2	—
Jersey	35.3	—
Liberia	61.1	—
Malta	0.5	—
Marshall Islands	339.8	—
Mauritius	4.2	—
Netherland Antilles	8.9	—

Source: CRS calculations, see text.

Notes: Dashes indicate data not available. Using 2008 earnings shares were 23.6% in Guernsey, 21.8% in Jersey, 31.0% in Liberia, 1.1% in Malta, and 6.6% in Mauritius. Based on the combined GDP in Curacao and St. Maartin, the share for the Netherland Antilles grew to 24%.

These data suggest not only a significant amount of profit shifting but also a notable change. The share of pretax profits reported by controlled foreign corporations in countries identified as tax havens in **Table 1** plus the Netherlands and reported in both years increased from 44% in 2004 to 59% in 2010, an increase of one-third.

Evidence of profit shifting has been presented in many other studies. Grubert and Altshuler report that profits of controlled foreign corporations in manufacturing relative to sales in Ireland are three times the group mean.[63] GAO reported higher shares of pretax profits of U.S. multinationals than of value added, tangible assets, sales, compensation, or employees in low-tax countries such as Bermuda, Ireland, the UK Caribbean, Singapore, and Switzerland.[64] Costa and Gravelle reported similar results for tax havens using subsequent data.[65] Martin Sullivan reports the return on assets for 1998 averaged 8.4% for U.S. manufacturing subsidiaries, but with returns of 23.8% in Ireland, 17.9% in Switzerland, and 16.6% in the Cayman Islands.[66] More recently, he noted that of the 10 countries that accounted for the most foreign multinational profits, the 5 countries with the highest manufacturing returns for 2004 (the Netherlands, Bermuda, Ireland, Switzerland, and China) all had effective tax rates below 12% while the 5 countries with lower returns (Canada, Japan, Mexico, Australia, and the United Kingdom) had effective tax rates in excess of 23%.[67] A number of econometric studies of this issue have been done.[68]

Estimates of the Cost and Sources of Corporate Tax Avoidance

There are no official estimates of the cost of international corporate tax avoidance, although a number of researchers have made estimates, nor are there official estimates of the individual tax gap.[69] In general, the estimates are not reflected in the overall tax gap estimate. The magnitude of corporate tax avoidance has been estimated through a variety of techniques and not all are for total avoidance. Some address only avoidance by U.S. multinationals and not by foreign parents of U.S. subsidiaries. Some focus only on a particular source of avoidance.[70]

Estimates of the potential revenue cost of income shifting by multinational corporations vary considerably, with some estimates in excess of $100 billion annually. The only study by the IRS in this area is an estimate of the international gross tax gap (not accounting for increased taxes collected on audit) related to transfer pricing based on audits of returns. They estimated a cost of about $3 billion, based on examinations of tax returns for 1996-1998.[71] This estimate would reflect an estimate not of legal avoidance, but of non-compliance, and for reasons stressed in the study has a number of limitations. One of those is that an audit does not detect all non- compliance, and it would not detect avoidance mechanisms which are, or appear to be, legal.

Some idea of the potential magnitude of the revenue lost from profit shifting by U.S. multinationals might be found in the estimates of the revenue gain from eliminating deferral. If most of the profit in low-tax countries has been shifted there to avoid U.S. tax rates, the projected revenue gain from ending deferral would provide an idea of the general magnitude of the revenue cost of profit shifting by U.S. parent firms. The Joint Committee on Taxation projected the revenue loss from deferral to be $83.5 billion in FY2014.[72] The Administration's estimates for ending deferral were smaller at $63.4 billion.[73] These estimates could be either an overstatement or an understatement of the cost of tax avoidance. They could be overstated because some of the profits abroad accrue to real investments in countries that have lower tax rates than the United States and thus do not reflect artificial shifting. They could be an understatement because they do not reflect the tax that could be collected by the United States rather than foreign jurisdictions on profits shifted to low-tax countries. For example, Ireland has a tax rate of 12.5% and the United States has a 35% rate, so ending deferral (absent behavioral changes) would only collect the excess of the U.S. tax over the Irish tax on shifted revenues, or about two-thirds of lost revenue.

Altshuler and Grubert estimated for 2002 that the corporate tax could be cut to 28% if deferral were ended, and based on corporate revenue in that year the gain was about $11 billion.[74] That year was at a low point because of the recession; if the share had remained the same, the gain would have been around $26 billion for FY2014.[75] The projection of the effects of deferral in tax expenditures has increased much faster than revenues, however.

Researchers have looked at differences in pretax returns and estimated the revenue gain if returns were equated. This approach should provide some estimates of the magnitude of overall profit shifting for multinationals, whether through transfer pricing, leveraging, or some other technique. Martin Sullivan, using Commerce Department data, estimates that, based on differences in pretax returns, the cost for 2004 was between $10 billion and $20 billion. Sullivan subsequently reports an estimated $17 billion increase in revenue loss from profit shifting between 1999 and 2004, which suggests that earlier number may be too small.[76] Sullivan suggests that the growth in profit shifting may be due to check-the-box. Sullivan subsequently estimated a $28 billion loss for 2007 which he characterized as conservative.[77] Charles Christian and Thomas Schultz, using rate of return on assets data from tax returns, estimated $87 billion was shifted in 2001, which, at a 35% tax rate, would imply a revenue loss of about $30 billion.[78] Adjusted proportionally to revenue, that amount would be $70 billion in 2014. As a guide for potential revenue loss from avoidance, these estimates suffer from two limits. The first is the inability to determine how much was shifted out of high-tax foreign jurisdictions rather than the United States, which leads to a range of estimates. At the same time, if capital is mobile, economic theory indicates that the returns should be lower, the lower the tax rate. Thus the results could also understate the overall profit shifting and the revenue loss to the United States.

Simon Pak and John Zdanowicz examined export and import prices, and estimated that lost revenue due to transfer pricing of goods alone was $53 billion in 2001.[79] This estimate should cover both U.S. multinationals and U.S. subsidiaries of foreign parents, but is limited to one technique. Kimberly Clausing, using regression techniques on cross-country data, which estimated profits reported as a function of tax rates, estimated that revenues of over $60 billion are lost for 2004 by applying a 35% tax rate to an estimated $180 billion in corporate profits shifted out of the United States.[80] She estimates that the profit-shifting effects are twice as large as the effects from shifts in actual economic activity. This methodological approach differs from others that involve direct calculations based on returns or prices and is subject to the econometric limitations with cross-country panel regressions. In theory, however, it had an overall of coverage of shifting (that is both outbound by U.S. parents of foreign corporations and inbound by foreign parents of U.S. corporations and covering all techniques).

Clausing and Reuven Avi-Yonah estimate the revenue gain from moving to a formula apportionment based on sales that is on the order of $50 billion per year because the fraction of worldwide income in the United States is smaller than the fraction of worldwide sales.[81] While this estimate is not an estimate of the loss from profit shifting (since sales and income could differ for other reasons), it is suggestive of the magnitude of total effects from profit shifting. A similar result was found by another study that applied formula apportionment based on an equal weight of assets, payroll, and sales.[82]

A more recent study by Clausing indicated that the revenue loss from profit shifting may have been as high as $90 billion in 2008, although an alternative data set indicates profit shifting of $57 billion.[83] For the last five years, the first method yielded losses ranging from 20% to 30% of profits. Using the second method, the range was 13% to 20%. If rising proportional to revenue, the 2014 level would be $66 billion to $104 billion.

Gabriel Zucman, using two different methodologies, found the revenue cost for profit shifting could range from $55 billion to $133 billion for 2013.[84] The lower number is from estimating the share of profits booked in tax havens and not repatriated, which would be assumed to be taxed fully if made subject to U.S. taxes. The second examines the decline in effective tax rate over time, and the residual, after accounting for other factors (about two-thirds), is attributed to profit shifting.

It is very difficult to develop a separate estimate for U.S. subsidiaries of foreign multinational companies because there is no way to observe the parent firm and its other subsidiaries. Several studies have documented that these firms have lower taxable income and that some have higher debt to asset ratios than domestic firms. There are many other potential explanations these differing characteristics, however, and domestic firms that are used as comparisons also have incentives to shift profits when they have foreign operations. No quantitative estimate has been made.[85] However some evidence of earnings stripping for inverted firms was found.[86]

Importance of Different Profit Shifting Techniques

Some studies have attempted to identify the importance of techniques used for profit shifting. Grubert has estimated that about half of income shifting was due to transfer pricing of intangibles and most of the remainder to shifting of debt.[87] In a subsequent study, Altshuler and Grubert find that multinationals saved $7 billion more between 1997 and 2002 due to check-the-box rules.[88] Some of this gain may have been at the cost of high-tax host countries rather than the United States, however.

Some of the estimates discussed here conflict with respect to the source of profit shifting. The Pak and Zdanowich estimates suggest that transfer pricing of goods is an important mechanism of tax avoidance, whereas Grubert suggests that the main methods of profit shifting are due to leverage and intangibles. The estimates for pricing of goods may, however, reflect errors, or money laundering motives rather than tax motives. Much of the shifting was associated with trade with high-tax countries; for example, Japan, Canada, and Germany accounted for 18% of the total.[89] At the same time, about 14% of the estimate reflected transactions with countries that appear on tax haven lists: the Netherlands, Taiwan, Singapore, Hong Kong, and Ireland.

A study by Jost Hekemeyer and Michael Overesch based on an analysis of 25 empirical studies found that transfer pricing was considerably more important than debt, accounting for an estimated 72% of the total, although their review covered studies on non-U.S. multinationals.[90] The growing importance of firms holding substantial intangible assets may point to a growing important of transfer pricing of intangibles. Hekemeyer and Overesch also found that reported profits on average decrease by 0.8% with a one percentage point change in the tax differential between two locations.

Some evidence that points to the importance of intangibles and the associated profits in tax haven countries can be developed by examining the sources of dividends repatriated during the "repatriation holiday" enacted in 2004.[91] This provision allowed, for a temporary period, dividends to be repatriated with an 85% deduction, leading to a tax rate of 5.25%. The pharmaceutical and medicine industry accounted for $99 billion in repatriations or 32% of the total. The computer and electronic equipment industry accounted for $58 billion or 18% of the total. Thus these two industries, which are high tech firms, accounted for half of the repatriations. The benefits were also highly concentrated in a few firms. According to a recent study, five firms (Pfizer, Merck, Hewlett-Packard, Johnson & Johnson, and IBM) are responsible for $88 billion, over a quarter (28%) of total repatriations.[92] The top 10 firms (adding Schering-Plough, Du Pont, Bristol-Myers Squibb, Eli Lilly, and PepsiCo) accounted for 42%. The top 15 (adding Procter and Gamble, Intel, Coca-Cola, Altria, and Motorola) accounted for over half (52%). These are firms that tend to, in most cases, have intangibles either in technology or brand names.

Finally, as shown in **Table 5**, which lists all countries accounting for at least 1% of the total of eligible dividends (and accounting for 87% of the total), most of the dividends were repatriated from countries that appear on tax haven lists.

METHODS OF AVOIDANCE AND EVASION BY INDIVIDUALS

Individual evasion of taxes may take different forms, and they are all facilitated by the growing international financial globalization and ease of making transactions on the Internet. Individuals can purchase foreign investments directly (outside the United States), such as stocks and bonds, or put money in foreign bank accounts and simply not report the income (although it is subject to tax under U.S. tax law). There has been little or no withholding information on individual taxpayers for this type of action. They could also use structures such as trusts or shell corporations to evade tax on investments, including investments made in the United States, which may take advantage of U.S. tax laws that exempt interest income and capital gains of non-residents from U.S. tax. Rather than using withholding or information collection the United States has largely relied in the past on the Qualified Intermediary (QI) program where beneficial owners are not revealed. To the extent any information gathering from other countries is done it is through bilateral information exchanges rather than multilateral information sharing. The European Union had developed a multilateral agreement but the United States does not participate.

New developments in information exchange may affect individual tax evasion both in the United States and abroad. In 2010, Congress enacted the Foreign Account Tax Compliance Act (FATCA) as part of the Hiring Incentives to Restore Employment Act (HIRE; P.L. 111-147).[93] FATCA recently become effective and requires foreign financial institutions to report information on asset holders or be subject to a 30% withholding rate. Its effectiveness is yet to be determined, although revenue projections when enacted did not predict a significant effect.

Table 5. Source of Dividends from "Repatriation Holiday": Countries Accounting for At Least 1% of Dividends

Country	Percentage of Total
Netherlands	28.8
Switzerland	10.4
Bermuda	10.2
Ireland	8.2
Luxembourg	7.5
Canada	5.9
Cayman Islands	5.9
United Kingdom	5.1
Hong Kong	1.7
Singapore	1.7
Malaysia	1.2

Source: Internal Revenue Service.

More recently, 51 other countries signed a multi-lateral information exchange agreement that set reporting standards which should eventually lead to fuller exchange of tax information by most countries.[94]

Tax Provisions Affecting the Treatment of Income by Individuals

The ability of U.S. persons (whether firms or individuals) to avoid tax on U.S. source income that they would normally be subject to arises from U.S. rules that do not impose withholding taxes on many sources of income. In general interest and capital gains are not subject to withholding. Dividends, non-portfolio interest (such as interest payments by a U.S. subsidiary to its parent), capital gains connected with a trade or business, and certain rents are subject to tax, although treaty arrangements widely reduce or eliminate the tax on dividends. In addition, even when dividends are potentially subject to a withholding tax, new techniques have developed to transform, through derivatives, those assets into exempt interest.[95]

The elimination of tax on interest income was unilaterally initiated by the United States in 1984, and other countries began to follow suit.[96] Currently, fears of capital flight are likely to keep countries from changing this treatment. However, it has been accompanied with a lack of information reporting and lack of information sharing that allows U.S. citizens, who are liable for these taxes, to avoid them whether on income invested abroad or income invested in the United States channeled through shell corporations and trusts. Citizens of foreign countries can also evade the tax, and the U.S. practice of not collecting information contributes to the problem.

Based on actual tax cases, Guttenberg and Avi-Yonah describe a typical way that U.S. individuals can easily evade tax on domestic income through a Cayman Islands operation with little expense using current technology. The individual, using the Internet, can open a bank account in the name of a Cayman corporation that can be set up for a minimal fee. Money can be electronically transferred without any reporting to tax authorities, and investments can be made in the United States or abroad. Investments by non-residents in interest bearing assets and most capital gains are not subject to a withholding tax in the United States.[97]

In addition to corporations, foreign trusts can be used to accomplish the same approach. Trusts may involve a trust protector who is an intermediary between the grantor and the trustees, but whose purpose may actually be to carry out the desires of the grantor. Some taxpayers argue that these trusts are legal but in either case they can be used to protect income from taxes, including those invested in the United States, from tax, while retaining control over and use of the funds.

Limited Information Reporting between Jurisdictions

In the past, the international taxation of passive portfolio income by individuals has been easily subject to evasion because there was no multilateral reporting of interest income. Even in those cases in which bilateral information sharing treaties, referred to as Tax Information Exchange Agreements (TIEAs) were in place, they had limits. As pointed out by Avi-Yonah, most of these agreements are restricted to criminal matters, which are a minor part of the revenues involved and pose difficult issues of evidence. Also, these agreements sometimes require that the activities related to the information being sought constitute crimes in both countries, which can be a substantial hurdle in cases of tax evasion. The OECD has adopted a model agreement with the *dual criminality* requirements.[98] TIEAs usually allow for information only upon request, requiring the United States and other countries to identify the potential tax evaders in advance and they do not override bank secrecy laws.

In some cases the countries themselves have little or no information of value. One article, for example, discussing the possibility of an information exchange agreement with the British Virgin Islands, a country with more than 400,000 registered corporations, where laws require no identification of shareholders or directors, and require no financial records, noted: "Even if the BVI signs an information exchange agreement, it is not clear what information could be exchanged."[99]

U.S. Collection of Information on U.S. Income and Qualified Intermediaries

Under the QI program, the United States did not require U.S. financial institutions to identify the true beneficiaries of interest and exempt dividends. The IRS set up a QI program in 2001, under which foreign banks that received payments certify the nationality of their depositors and reveal the identity of any U.S. citizens.[100] However, although QIs are supposed to certify nationality,[101] apparently some relied on self-certification.[102] QIs are also subject to audit. However, UBS, the Swiss bank involved in a tax abuse scandal that helped clients set up offshore plans, was a QI, and that event raised some questions about the QI program.

A nonqualified intermediary must disclose the identity of its customers to obtain the exemption for passive income such as interest and or the reduced rates arising from tax treaties, but there are also questions about the accuracy of disclosures.

The FATCA provisions in P.L. 111-147 strengthened the rules affecting qualified intermediaries' identification of asset holders, with backup withholding provisions. The projected revenue gain was quite small (less than $1 billion per year) relative to projected costs (discussed below).

European Union Savings Directive

The European Union, in its savings directive, has developed among its members an option of either information reporting or a withholding tax. The reporting or withholding option covers the member countries as well as some other countries. Three states, Austria, Belgium, and Luxembourg, have elected the withholding tax. While this multilateral agreement aids these countries' tax administration, the United States is not a participant.

Estimates of the Revenue Cost of Individual Tax Evasion

A number of different approaches have been used to estimate corporate tax avoidance, however, all of these approaches rely on data reported on assets and income. For individual evasion, estimates are much more difficult because the initial basis of the estimate is the amount of assets held abroad whose income is not reported to the tax authorities. In addition to this estimate, the expected rate of return and tax rate are needed to estimate the revenue cost.

Joseph Guttentag and Avi-Yonah estimate a value of $50 billion in individual tax evasion, based on an estimate of holdings by high net worth individuals invested outside the United States at $1.5 trillion.[103] Using a rate of return of 10% and a tax rate of approximately one-third, they obtain an estimate of $50 billion. They also summarize two other estimates in 2002 of $40 billion for the international tax gap by the IRS and $70 billion by an IRS consultant.

To the extent that the earnings are interest, the 10% rate of return may be too high, while if it is dividends and capital gains, the tax rate is too high. Using a tax rate of 15% (currently applicable to capital gains and dividends) would lead to about $23 billion. In the case of equity investments, if a third of the return is in dividends and half of capital gains is never realized, the tax rate would be 10% or about $15 billion assuming the 10% return. During 2002 and beginning in 2011, however, the tax rate on capital gains and dividends is 20%, indicating a loss of $20 billion rather than $15 billion. For interest, since investors can earn tax free returns in the neighborhood of 4% to 5% on domestic state and local bonds, to yield a 5% after-tax return at a 35% tax rate would require a pretax yield of about 7.7%. The estimate would then be $40 billion.

The Tax Justice Network has estimated a worldwide revenue loss for all countries of $255 billion from individual tax evasion, basically using a 7.5% return and a 30% tax rate.[104] These assumptions would be consistent with a $33 billion loss for the United States using the $1.5 trillion figure. Their worldwide numbers are consistent with $11 trillion in offshore wealth. Their more recent estimates place wealth at $21 trillion to $32 trillion, which would double or triple these estimates.[105] Thus the cost for the United States could be much larger approaching $100 billion.

Zucman estimates $1.2 trillion in U.S. financial wealth abroad based on anomalies in investment data, with an estimated tax loss of $36 billion in

2013.[106] There is no way to know whether the high-profile cases of prosecuting individuals, tax amnesty, or the imminent arrival of FATCA might have reduced these amounts of wealth.

Alternative Policy Options to Address Corporate Profit Shifting

Because much of the corporate tax revenue loss arises from activities that either are legal or appear to be so, it is difficult to address these issues other than with changes in the tax law. Outcomes would likely be better if there is international cooperation. Currently, the possibilities for international cooperation appear to play a bigger role in options for dealing with individual evasion than with corporate avoidance.

Several of the issues addressed below, such as hybrid entities and instruments, transfer pricing for intangibles, and debt also have been considered in the OECD action plan on base erosion and profit shifting.[107]

Broad Changes to International Tax Rules

The first set of provisions would introduce broad changes in international tax rules, and include significant restrictions in deferral or allocation of income and capital.

Repeal Deferral

One approach to mitigate the rewards of profit shifting is to repeal deferral, or to institute true worldwide taxation of foreign source income. Firms would be subject to current tax on the income of their foreign subsidiaries, although they would continue to be able to take foreign tax credits. According to estimates cited above, this change currently would raise from $63.4 billion to $83.4 billion per year.

Many of the issues surrounding the repeal of deferral have focused on the real effects of repeal on the allocation of capital. Traditionally, economic analysis has suggested that eliminating deferral would increase economic efficiency, although recently some have argued that this gain would be offset by the loss of production of some efficient firms from high-tax countries. Some have also argued for retaining the current system or moving in the other direction to a territorial tax. These economic issues are discussed in detail in another CRS report.[108]

Repeal of deferral would largely eliminate the value of the planning techniques discussed in this report. There are concerns, however, that firms could avoid the effects of repeal by having their parent incorporate in other countries that continue to allow deferral. The most direct and beneficial to reducing firms' tax liabilities of these planning approaches, inversion, has been addressed by legislation in 2004.[109] Mergers would be another method to counter the implementation of deferral, although mergers involve real changes in organization that would not likely be undertaken to gain a small tax benefit. Another possibility is that more direct portfolio investment (i.e., buying shares of stock by individual investors) in foreign corporations will occur. There has been a significant growth in this direct investment, although the evidence suggests this investment has been due to portfolio diversification and not tax avoidance.[110]

S. 767, a broad tax reform bill introduced by Senators Wyden and Coats in the 112th Congress, would have eliminated deferral. In the 113th Congress, H.R. 694 (Representative Schakowsky) and S. 250 (Senator Sanders), also would have eliminated deferral.

Targeted or Partial Elimination of Deferral

More narrow proposals to address deferral and tax avoidance would tax income in tax havens currently or some additional income of foreign subsidiaries. They include

- eliminating deferral for specified tax havens;
- eliminating deferral in countries with tax rates that are below the U.S. rate by a specified proportion;
- eliminating deferral for income on the production of goods that are imported into the United States;
- eliminating deferral for income on the production of goods that are exported, requiring a minimum payout share; and
- taxing currently at a lower minimum rate.

Restricting current taxation to tax havens would likely address some of the problems associated with transfer pricing and leveraging, without ending deferral entirely. Defining a tax haven under those circumstances would be crucial. A bill introduced in the 110th Congress, S. 396, which defined as a U.S. firm any U.S. subsidiary in a tax haven not engaged in an active business, had a list of countries that was the same as the original OECD tax haven list, except for the U.S. Virgin Islands. Some countries that are often considered tax havens, would not be subject to such provisions, leaving some scope for corporate tax avoidance. In addition, firms could shift some operations to other lower tax countries and increase the amount of foreign tax credits available, which would be a loss to U.S. revenue. Some concerns have also been expressed that listing specific tax haven countries would make cooperative approaches, such as tax information sharing treaties, more difficult.

An alternative, which would not require identifying particular countries, would be to restrict deferral based on a tax rate that is lower than the U.S. rate by a specified amount. For example, the French, who generally have a territorial tax, tax income earned in jurisdictions with tax rates one-third lower than the French rate. For the United States, whose tax rate is similar to the French rate, this ratio would indicate a tax rate lower than 24%.

Another proposal directed to runaway plans would eliminate deferral for investments abroad that produce exports into the United States. S. 1284, also in the 110th Congress, would have imposed current taxation on such activities by expanding Subpart F income to include income attributable to imports into the United States of goods produced by foreign subsidiaries of U.S. firms. The main problem with this proposal is administering it, which would include tracing selling to a third party for resale.

A somewhat different and more restrictive proposal was made by Senator Kerry during the 2004 presidential campaign. He proposed to eliminate deferral except in cases in which income is produced and sold in the controlled foreign corporation's jurisdiction. This approach would, like deferral in general, be likely to significantly restrict opportunities for artificial profit shifting, because most of the income in tax haven or low-tax jurisdictions does not arise from real activity; indeed, these jurisdictions are too small in many cases to provide a market. As with the previous proposal, however, the administration of such a plan would be difficult.

An option that would not go as far as eliminating deferral altogether would be to require some minimum share to be paid out. A related option would be to tax income currently but at a minimum rate that is lower than the U.S. rate. Then-Chairman Baucus of the Senate Finance Committee released, in 2013, a discussion draft of a proposal that would have taxed foreign source income when earned at rates 60% or 80% of the statutory rate.[111] The 60% and 80% were only suggestions at this point. The President has also suggested minimum tax approaches, without providing specifics.[112] Chairman Camp's tax reform proposal in the 113th Congress (S. 1) includes a minimum tax on intangible income as part of anti-abuse provisions in moving to a territorial tax system.

Allocation of Deductions and Credits with Respect to Deferred Income/Restrictions on Cross Crediting

A proposal that does not end deferral but makes the shifting of profits from high-tax countries less attractive is a provision to allocate deductions and credits, so as to deny those benefits until income is repatriated. This approach was included in a tax reform bill introduced by Chairman Rangel of the Ways and Means Committee in 2007 (H.R. 3970) and is included in the current proposals by President Obama. Under this proposal, a portion of certain overall deductions, such as interest or overhead, that reflects the share of foreign deferred income, would be disallowed. The foreign tax credit allocation rule would allow credits for the share of foreign taxes paid that are equal to the share of foreign source income repatriated. Disallowed deductions and credits would be carried forward. (President Obama's proposal does not allocate research and experimental expenses.)

The allocation-of-deductions provision would decrease the tax benefits of sheltering income in low-tax jurisdictions and encourage repatriation of income relative to current law and presumably reduce profit shifting, as well as decrease benefits of real investment abroad. The foreign tax credit allocation rule could have a variety of effects. It would make foreign investment abroad less attractive because it would increase the tax on income when eventually repatriated. It also would discourage investment in low-tax jurisdictions that could no longer be sheltered by foreign tax credits and discourage repatriation of earnings on existing activities because of the potential tax to be collected.

The allocation of credits accomplishes some of the restrictions on cross crediting that could also be achieved by increasing the number of baskets. As discussed below, one possible separate basket would be for active royalties. Another possibility would be to impose a per country limit with a separate basket for each country (and baskets within each for passive, active, etc., income). S. 3018, a broad tax reform bill introduced by Senators Wyden and Gregg in the 111th Congress, and a similar bill, S. 727, introduced by Senators Wyden and Coats in the 112th Congress, would have provided for a per country limit, as would have H.R. 694 (Representative Schakowsy) and S. 250 (Senator Sanders) in the 113th Congress.

Formula Apportionment

Another approach to addressing income shifting is through formula apportionment, which would be a major change in the international tax system. With formula apportionment, income would be allocated to different jurisdictions based on their shares of some combination of sales, assets, and employment. This approach is used by many states in the United States and by the Canadian provinces to allocate income. (In the past, a three factor apportionment was used, but some states have moved to a sales based system.) Studies have estimated a significant increase in taxes from adopting formula apportionment. Slemrod and Shackleford estimate a 38% revenue increase from an equally weighted three-factor system.[113] A sales-based formula has been proposed by Avi- Yonah and Clausing that they estimate would raise about 35% of additional corporate revenue, or $50 billion annually over the 2001-2004 period.[114]

The ability of a formula apportionment system to address some of the problems of shifting income becomes problematic with intangible assets.[115] If all capital were tangible capital, such as buildings and equipment, a formula apportionment system based on capital would at least lead to the same rate of return for tax purposes across high-tax and low-tax jurisdictions. Real distortions in the allocation of capital would remain, since capital would still flow to low-tax jurisdictions, but paper profits could not be shifted. An allocation system based on assets becomes more difficult when intangible assets are involved. It is probably as difficult to estimate the stock of intangible investment (given lack of information on the future pattern of profitability) as it is to allocate it under arms-length pricing. In the case of an allocation based on sales, profits that might appropriately be associated with domestic income as they arise from domestic investment in R&D would be allocated abroad. Moreover, new avenues of tax planning, such as selling to an intermediary in a low-tax country for resale, would complicate the administration of such a plan. Whether the benefits are greater than the costs is in some dispute.[116]

One problem is that if the United States adopted the system there could be double taxation of some income and no taxation of other income unless there were a multinational plan. The European Union has been considering a formula apportionment applied to its member states, based on property, gross receipts, number of employees and cost of employment.[117] This proposal and the consequences for different countries are discussed by Devereux and Loretz.[118] If the European Union adopted such a plan it would be easier for the

United States to adopt a similar apportionment formula without as much risk of double or no taxation with respect to its major trading partners.

Narrower Provisions Affecting Multinational Profit Shifting

Various more narrow provisions could be considered that would be more focused on preventing abuses and have fewer consequences for the overall structure of international corporate taxation. Note that P.L. 111-226 addresses a number of problems with the foreign tax credit; these changes are summarized below along with other legislation in 2011 relating to international tax avoidance and evasion.

Eliminate Check-the-Box, Hybrid Entities, and Hybrid Instruments

A number of proposals have been made to eliminate check-the-box and in general to adopt rules that would require legal entities to be characterized in a consistent manner by the United States and the country in which an entity is established. This proposal has been made by McIntyre.[119] Rules requiring that legal entities be characterized in a consistent manner by the United States and by the country in which they are established and that tax benefits arising from inconsistent treatment of instruments be denied would address this particular class of provisions that undermine Subpart F and the matching of credits and deductions with income. President Obama's first budget proposal included a provision that disallows a subsidiary to treat a subsidiary chartered in another country as a disregarded entity.

Tighten Earnings Stripping Rules; Limit Interest Deductions

In the American Jobs Creation Act of 2004, a further restriction on earnings stripping rules was considered as an alternative to the anti-inversion measure. These provisions were not enacted but were to be studied in a Treasury report. The 2004 House proposal would have raised revenue by dropping the debt-to-asset share test and lowering the interest share standard to 25% for ordinary debt, 50% for guaranteed debt, and 30% overall. In general, further restrictions on earnings stripping could be considered to address shifting through debt for U.S. subsidiaries of foreign parents.

President Obama's budget proposals include a more restrictive rule for multinational firms, allocating interest across the firm's related groups in proportion to earnings.[120] Allocation rules were also included in Chairman Camp's Tax Reform Proposal in the 113th Congress (H.R. 1).

Foreign Tax Credits: Source Royalties as Domestic Income for Purposes of the Foreign Tax Credit Limit or Create Separate Basket; Eliminate Title Passage Rule; Restrict Credits for Taxes Producing an Economic Benefit

As noted above, one of the issues surrounding the cross-crediting of the foreign tax credit is the use of excess credits to shield royalties from U.S. tax on income that could be considered U.S. source income. Two options might be considered to address that issue: sourcing these royalties as domestic income for purposes of the credit or putting them into a separate foreign tax credit basket.[121] The same issue applies to the provision that allows half of the income from exports to be allocated to the country in which the title passes. President Obama's proposal includes a provision to restrict the crediting of taxes that are in exchange for an economic benefit (such as payments that are the equivalent of royalties).

Transfer Pricing

Michael McIntyre has suggested some other proposals to deal with transfer pricing, which include making transfer pricing penalties nearly automatic for taxpayers who have not kept contemporaneous records. He also suggests use of some type of formula apportionment plan as a default for transfer pricing for non-complying taxpayers so the IRS does not have to conduct a detailed transaction by transaction assessment for the court.

President Obama's budget proposals would address some of the transfer pricing issues associated with the transfer of intangibles by clarifying that intangibles include workforce in place, goodwill, and going concern value and that they are valued at their highest and best use. The plan would allow the IRS commissioner to aggregate intangibles if that leads to a more appropriate value.

These proposals would likely have small effects. Any significant solution to the transfer pricing problem, especially for intangibles, is difficult to entertain short of an elimination of deferral.

The President's budget proposals also included a more significant proposal to treat excess returns on intangibles in a low-tax country as Subpart F income (and therefore not subject to deferral) and to place it in a separate foreign tax credit basket. If such an approach could be successfully implemented, it might have important consequences for transfer pricing using intangibles.

Other Provisions

There are numerous other proposals that often have a narrow focus, such as on methods of avoiding taxes on repatriation and shifting headquarters. These provisions are discussed as a part of proposed legislation in the final section of this report.

OPTIONS TO ADDRESS INDIVIDUAL EVASION

Most of the options for addressing individual evasion involve more information reporting and additional enforcement. There are options that would involve fundamental changes in the law, such as shifting from a residence to a source basis for passive income. That is, the United States would tax this passive income earned in its borders, just as is the case for corporate and other active income. This change involves, however, many other economic and efficiency effects that are probably not desirable. The remainder of the proposals discussed here do not involve any fundamental changes in the tax itself, but rather focus on administration and enforcement.

The options discussed below are drawn from many sources, including academics and practitioners, organizations, and the Internal Revenue Service, and contained in legislative proposals; citations to these sources are provided at this point and legislative proposals are summarized in the next section.[122]

Subsequent sections explain proposals that were adopted in the HIRE Act, P.L. 111-147.

Information Reporting

Expanded information reporting can involve multilateral efforts, changes in the current bilateral treaties, or unilateral changes.

Multilateral Information Sharing or Withholding; International Cooperation

The European Union Directive, which would require information reporting (or withholding), is one example of a multilateral approach to information reporting. Avi-Yonah and Avi-Yonah and Guttentag have suggested that current Treasury policy is to focus on bilateral agreements to achieve information exchange, but that the United States should also focus on cooperation with the OECD and G-20 and other appropriate organizations to improve information and persuade tax havens to enter into exchanges based on the OECD model. Shay suggests this approach as well and particularly references electronic information exchange.

The Tax Justice Network has proposed that the United Nations develop a global tax cooperation standard, set up a panel to determine compliant states, and deny recognition to non-compliant jurisdictions. They have also suggested that the IMF and World Bank country assessments address tax compliance.

Expanding Bilateral Information Exchange

A number of commentators have suggested an increase in the scope of bilateral information treaties to provide for regular and automatic exchanges of information. This would require the U.S. banks to increase their collection of information.

Avi-Yonah and Avid-Yonah and Guttentag suggest adopting the model OECD bilateral Tax Information Exchange Agreement (TIEA). This information exchange would relate to civil as well as criminal issues, it would not require suspicion of a crime other than tax evasion, and would override tax haven bank secrecy laws. Non-tax havens could be induced to make such agreements to obtain information, and thus, such a change would require collection of information on interest payments by banks and financial institutions. Treasury has proposed only 16 countries, but Avi-Yonah and Guttenberg suggest no reason to restrict the provision in this way. Treasury could use existing authority not to exchange information that might be misused by non-democratic foreign governments.

Unilateral Approaches: Withholding/Refund Approach; Increased Information Reporting Requirements

This step is one that the United States could undertake without multilateral or bilateral cooperation, namely imposing withholding taxes on interest income and other exempt income received from U.S. sources by foreign intermediaries and providing a refund upon proof that the beneficial recipient was eligible. Avi-Yonah suggests this change with the hope that it would be adopted multilaterally.

A variation of this approach would be to require disclosure of the names of customers including beneficial owners, with withholding imposed if disclosure was not forthcoming as adopted in the HIRE Act, discussed subsequently.

Other Measures That Might Improve Compliance

Incentives/Sanctions for Tax Havens

Avi-Yonah and Avi-Yonah and Guttenberg suggest a carrot and stick approach to tax havens. They argue that little of the benefit of tax havens flows to their sometimes needy residents, but rather to the professionals providing banking and legal services, who often live elsewhere. They suggest transitional aid to move away from these offshore activities. For non-cooperating tax havens, they suggest the Treasury use its existing authority to deny benefits of the interest exemption. They suggest that tax havens cannot continue to exist unless the wealthy countries permit it, because funds are not productive in tax havens.

The Stop Tax Haven Abuse Act would extend to tax enforcement the sanctions of the Patriot Act used to impose penalties for money laundering and terrorist financing. Sanctions vary in severity and range from increased reporting on transactions to prohibitions. Sullivan points out that the U.S. government has used the Patriot Act sparingly, however, and questions whether this change would be a credible threat.

Blessing suggests that sanctions should be multilateral rather than unilateral.

Revise and Strengthen the Qualified Intermediary Program

Several proposals relating to the QI program, which were discussed by witnesses at a Ways and Means Committee hearing on March 31, 2009, were reported by Sullivan. Some changes have already been made by FATCA (in the HIRE Act, discussed below).

Place the Burden of Proof on the Taxpayer

An important part of the Stop Tax Haven Abuse proposal is to place the burden of proof in court on the taxpayer; this approach was also suggested by Blum. As noted above, there is also a shift in the burden of proof for accounts with non-qualified intermediaries for filing an FBAR (Foreign Bank and Financial Account Report).

President Obama's proposal would create a presumption that the funds in foreign accounts are large enough to require an FBAR, which is required when amounts exceed $10,000. It would treat failure to file for amounts in excess of $200,000 as willful, which permits criminal penalties and larger civil penalties.

The HIRE Act (P.L. 111-147) would assume that, when adequate information is not provided, foreign accounts exceed the $50,000 minimum that requires reporting (under other provisions) on the tax return for purposes of assessing penalties.

Treat Shell Corporations as U.S. Firms

The Stop Tax Haven Abuse Act includes a provision to treat any firm that is publicly traded or has assets over $50 million as a U.S. corporation. This provision would include hedge funds but would not affect subsidiaries of multinational firms because decisions are made by the parent firm. Sullivan argues that such a provision would have a devastating effect on the U.S. hedge fund industry, where offshore firms generally attract tax exempt U.S. investors and foreigners who wish to avoid filing tax returns, as well as U.S. tax evaders, and that legislative relief for U.S. tax exempt investors (pension funds, university endowments) would be likely.

Extend the Statute of Limitations

Extensions in the statute of limitations are said by some to be needed due to the complexity of the international cases and difficulty of obtaining information. Extension has been proposed by numerous commentators, is supported by the IRS officials and is included in the proposed Stop Tax Haven Abuse Act, proposals discussed by the Senate Finance Committee, and proposals made by President Obama. These legislative proposals would extend the statute of limitations from 3 years to 6 years, but Blum also suggests the possibility of 10 years. The HIRE Act (P.L. 111-147) extends the statute of limitations to six years.

Greater Resources for the Internal Revenue Service to Focus on Offshore

Numerous suggestions have been made to expand IRS resources for combating overseas tax abuses. President Obama's proposal, for example, has proposed to fund 800 new positions to combat international abuses.

Blum says that agents should not be pressured to give up difficult cases because of short-term performance goals based on closing cases and collecting revenues.

Make Civil Cases Public as a Deterrent

Blum suggests all settlements involving offshore schemes in excess of $1 million should be excluded from the restrictions of Section 6103 that require settled civil cases to be confidential. He argues that no one knows about these cases and thus taxpayers think the possibility of being caught is small.

John Doe Summons

A provision in the proposed Stop Tax Haven Abuse Act would make it easier to issue John Doe summons where the IRS does not know the names of taxpayers and now must ask courts for permission to serve the summons. This section provides that in any case involving offshore secret accounts, the court is to presume tax compliance is at issue, to relieve the IRS of the obligation when the only records sought are U.S. bank records, and to issue John Doe summons for large investigative projects without addressing each set of summons separately.

Strengthening of Penalties

Increased penalties are included in the proposed Stop Tax Haven Abuse Act, the Finance Committee Draft and President Obama's proposals. Among the penalty provisions in various proposals are increased penalties for failure to file FBARs; basing the FBAR penalty on the highest amount in period rather than on a particular day; and increased penalties on abusive tax shelters, failure to file information on foreign trusts, and certain offshore transactions. President Obama's proposals would double accuracy-related penalties for foreign transactions and increase penalties for trusts and permit them to be imposed if the amount in the trust cannot be established; this provision was included in The HIRE Act (P.L. 111-147).

The proposed Stop Tax Haven Abuse Act also includes a provision that legal opinions that take the position that a transaction is more likely than not to prevail for tax purposes will no longer shield taxpayers from penalties.

S. 386, the Fraud Recovery and Investment Act, would introduce criminal penalties. Some tax attorneys have questioned whether these proposals are too harsh or might undermine amnesty or voluntary compliance.[123]

Address Tax Shelters

The proposed Stop Tax Haven Abuse Act would make a number of additional changes addressing tax shelters, including prohibiting the patenting of tax shelters, developing an examination procedure so that bank regulators could detect questionable tax activities, disallowing fees contingent on tax savings, removing communication barriers between enforcement agencies, codifying regulations, making it clear that prohibition of disclosure by tax preparers does not prevent congressional subpoenas, and providing standards for tax shelter opinion letters.

Regulate the Rules Used by States to Permit Incorporation

Blum suggests that all U.S. Limited Liability Companies (LLCs) have a taxpayer ID number, a requirement not imposed in Delaware and other states that keep no records of ownership. S. 569 would tighten regulations to require record-keeping and identification of beneficial owners of corporations and LLCs and commission a study of partnerships and trusts.

Make Suspicious Activity Reports Available to Civil Side of IRS

The proposal that information on suspicious activity reports filed by financial institutions under anti-money laundering acts be made available to the civil side of IRS was made by Blum, who indicated that agency policy at the top levels had prohibited this information sharing. It is included in a provision in the Stop Tax Haven Abuse Act.

Summary of Enacted Legislation in 2011

Three bills enacted in 2011 contain provisions relating to international compliance: the HIRE Act, the Affordable Care Act, and P.L. 111-226.[124]

The Hiring Incentives to Restore Employment (HIRE) Act (P.L. 111-147): FATCA

The foreign provisions in this act are projected to have a relatively small effect, $8.7 billion over 10 years, when compared with estimated costs of international evasion of around $40 billion a year. This section of the act is referred to as the Foreign Account Tax Compliance Act, or FATCA.

Reporting on Foreign Accounts

This provision would institute withholding on payments, at a 30% rate, to foreign financial institutions and other institutions unless certain information requirements are met. Although the provision allows considerable regulatory scope, the requirements include providing specific details on U.S. beneficial owners. The institution determines U.S. beneficial owners, with oversight by the Treasury.

Deduction of Interest for Bearer (Nonregistered) Bonds

Non-registered bonds (with some exceptions, including those issued by natural persons, not for public sale, or of maturities of less than a year) are subject to restrictions, including an excise tax and denial of interest deductions; there is an exception for foreign targeted bonds. Foreign- targeted bonds are designed to be sold to non-U.S. persons, payable outside of the United States, and containing a statement that any bond held by a U.S. person will be subject to U.S. tax laws. This provision repeals the foreign targeted bond exception for purposes of interest deductibility. Non-registered state and local bond interest for these bonds are also not eligible for tax exclusion.

Additional Information Reported on Tax Returns

Individuals who are required to file an FBAR (Foreign Bank and Financial Account Report) would also be required to report this information on the tax return if the amount in the account is $50,000 or more. For purposes of this report on the tax return, interests in foreign trusts would also be included. A presumption will be made that the amount of the account is at least $50,000 when no detailed information is provided.

Penalties

The 20% accuracy-related penalty that already applies is increased to 40% for transactions involving foreign accounts where the taxpayer failed to disclose reportable information. A reasonable cause exception would not be available. In the case of failure to report or under- reporting foreign trusts, the initial penalty is 35% of the trust amount (5% in certain cases). If the failure to report continues for 90 days, an additional penalty of $10,000 is imposed for each 30- day period, but the total cannot exceed the amount of the trust. This provision would change the initial penalty from 35% (5%) of the trust amount a minimum of $10,000. The $10,000 for each 30-day period is continued indefinitely, with a refund of any excess when the taxpayer does report. This proposal addresses the problem of the IRS not being able to assess a penalty because it cannot determine the amount in the account.

Statute of Limitations

The statute of limitations for cross-border transactions is extended from three to six years in instances where more than $5,000 of income is omitted.

Reporting on Foreign Passive Investment Companies

The legislation addresses reporting by passive foreign investment companies (PFICs) by codifying proposed regulations requiring shareholders to file annual information reports. The Secretary of the Treasury has regulatory authority over the type of information and can also provide for regulations that address duplicate reporting from other provisions in the legislation.

Electronic Filing

Electronic filing is required of persons who file at least 250 returns (including information returns). This legislation requires electronic filing for financial institutions regardless of whether the institution provides 250 returns, which would generally be relevant to foreign financial institutions.

Trusts

The legislation would further restrict foreign trusts by treating the grantor as the owner if there is a future contingency for a U.S. beneficiary or an agreement the grantor is involved in that might provide for a U.S. beneficiary. It also places the burden of proof on the grantor, treats a loan or use of property without appropriate compensation as a benefit, and requires information reporting.

Treat Equity Swaps as Dividends

This provision addresses the problem of disguising dividends that are subject to taxation as interest that is not. This provision, which would generally treat equity swaps as dividends, would raise $1.1 billion for FY2011-FY2020 according to the President's proposals.

Economic Substance Doctrine: The Patient Protection and Affordable Care Act, P.L. 111-148

The economic substance doctrine was adopted in the health reform legislation, P.L. 111-148. This provision, although general in nature, is relevant to international tax evasion and avoidance. Firms that enter into tax savings arrangements that are found not to have economic substance can have their tax benefits disallowed by the courts under what has become known as the economic substance doctrine. The doctrine is sometimes interpreted differently by different courts, and recent legislative proposals have sought to make the doctrine more uniform through statute. Generally, this provision requires a transaction to meet both an objective test (profit was made) and a subjective test (profit was intended). Penalties are also imposed. Supporters argue that the stricter test will not only reduce tax avoidance but also make treatment more consistent across the courts. Some tax attorneys are concerned that more specific rules might provide a roadmap to structuring arrangements that will pass the test.

P.L. 111-226

On May 20, 2010, the Ways and Means Committee Chairman Levin and Senate Finance Committee Baucus released a plan for combining Senate and House proposals for extending temporary tax benefits and providing for spending increases.[125] Among the revenue raisers were several foreign provisions largely relating to the foreign tax credit, which were developed jointly with the Treasury Department. Some are also included in the President's 2011 budget proposals. They would raise $14.451 billion over 10 years. These provisions were adopted as part of H.R. 4213 on May 28, 2010.

Some of these issues arise from the overall limit on the foreign tax credit, which allows aggregate foreign taxes paid abroad to be credited against U.S. tax on aggregate foreign earnings. Under these rules, firms are either in excess credit positions (they have foreign taxes that cannot be used because aggregate foreign taxes exceed aggregate U.S. tax on foreign source income) or in an excess limit position (they do not have enough foreign taxes to offset U.S. tax on foreign source income). In the former case, any technique that increases the amount of their income that is considered foreign source reduces overall tax because it increases the limit on foreign tax credits; in the latter case, any technique that allows recognition of foreign taxes without the accompanying income reduces taxes.

H.R. 4213 was not enacted, but a smaller spending bill using H.R. 1586 as a vehicle included most of the foreign provisions in H.R. 4213. H.R. 1586 provided money to the states for education and Medicaid funding, with costs paid for in part by these foreign revisions. It was signed into law on August 10, 2010. The provisions are summarized below.[126]

Preventing Splitting Foreign Tax Credits from Income

This provision addresses the issue of reverse hybrids and mechanisms that allow firms to recognize and take credits for foreign taxes paid without reporting the income that gave rise to the foreign taxes (discussed earlier in this report), thus using those credits to offset tax on unrelated income. The proposal would implement a matching rule so that foreign tax credits would not be recognized until the income is taken into account. This proposal is estimated to raise $6.325 billion over 10 years.

Denial of Foreign Tax credits for Covered Asset Acquisitions

Taxpayers can acquire a firm by purchasing stock or by purchasing the underlying assets. In the latter case, assets are valued at current market value, which generally increases depreciation deductions. Certain U.S. tax rules allow a stock acquisition to be treated as an asset acquisition. Foreign governments may not apply a similar rule. As a result, depreciation deductions under the foreign rules are smaller than under the U.S. rules, and income and foreign taxes paid are higher. The excess of foreign taxes over U.S. taxes on this transaction can be used to offset U.S. tax on unrelated foreign income under the overall foreign tax credit limitation. Such an outcome can also occur when taxpayers acquire entities that are partnerships for U.S. purposes and corporations for foreign tax purposes. The provision prevents firms from obtaining credits for these excess taxes. This proposal is estimated to raise $4.025 billion over 10 years.

Separate Foreign Tax Credit Limit for Items Resourced Under Treaties

Current tax treaties provide that some income that would normally be considered U.S. source income can be resourced in foreign countries. For example, interest paid on U.S. securities to a firm's foreign subsidiary would normally be U.S. source income, but under a treaty may be sourced in the foreign country. The foreign country may tax net interest (interest income less interest paid), but the entire gross interest payment would be considered foreign source and eligible for offsetting foreign tax credits. This increase in foreign source income could, absent other provisions, lead to tax reductions from excess foreign taxes on other income. Current law places this operation in a separate foreign tax credit basket when the foreign firm is a subsidiary of a U.S. firm incorporated abroad. This provision extends the treatment to branch operations and disregarded entities (that are treated the same as branches under check-the-box rules). The provision would apply to taxable years beginning after the date of enactment. This proposal is estimated to raise $253 million over 10 years.

Limitation on the Use of Section 956 (the "Hopscotch" Rule)

The hopscotch rules issue arises from the combination of two different tax provisions. The first is the treatment of dividends from foreign subsidiaries when there are multiple tiers of these subsidiaries. For example, a U.S. parent might have a subsidiary (tier 1), which in turn has a subsidiary (tier 2). If a tier 2 firm wants to pay a dividend to the parent, it would first be paid to the tier 1 subsidiary, which would in turn pay it to the parent. The foreign tax credit allowed would be a blend of the tax rate in the tier one subsidiary and the tier 2 subsidiary. For example, if one-half of the income of the tier 1 subsidiary was its own and the tax rate was 10% and one-half was from the payment from the tier 2 firm with a 50% tax rate, and dividend paid by the tier 1 subsidiary to the U.S. parent would have a 30% rate. These deemed taxes paid could be used for foreign tax credits against any U.S. tax on foreign source income. The second provision is Section 956, which was designed to prevent firms from returning income to the U.S. parent without paying tax, but using methods such as lending to the parent or buying property from the parent. A payment made in this fashion is construed as a dividend. Therefore, if the tier 2 subsidiary made a transaction that fell into the Section 956 rules, it could "hopscotch" over the tier 1 subsidiary and receive a full 50% tax rate: two-thirds larger than the 30% rate allowed under the blended credit rule. This provision preserves the blended rate in the case of Section 956 transactions. This proposal is estimated to raise $1.010 billion over 10 years.

Special Rule for Certain Redemptions by Foreign Subsidiaries

This issue relates to circumstances where a foreign multinational company owns a U.S. firm, which in turn owns a foreign subsidiary, and the foreign subsidiary purchases stock in the U.S. firm from the foreign multinational with cash. The cash payment can be considered a direct dividend payment to the foreign multinational up to the earnings and profits of the foreign subsidiary and thus bypasses the U.S. tax system. (If earnings and profits of the subsidiary are exhausted the payment comes from earnings and profits of the U.S. company and are subject to dividend withholding taxes unless exempted by treaty.) The earnings and profits of the foreign subsidiary are reduced by the amount of the payment so that they are not available for future taxation. If the foreign subsidiary had paid a dividend directly to the U.S. parent, it would have been subject to tax at the firm level and to a withholding tax on the dividend (unless exempted by treaty). This provision would not allow earnings and profits of the foreign subsidiary to be taken into account if more than 50% of the dividend would bypass the U.S. tax system. It is estimated to raise $255 million over 10 years.

Modification of Affiliation Rules for Allocating Interest Expense

Foreign tax credits are limited to the U.S. tax that would be due on foreign source income if taxed in the United States. In determining foreign source income, a share of the interest paid by the U.S. parent and related U.S. affiliates is assigned to foreign income based on the share of total assets that are foreign. The more interest that is assigned to foreign sources, the smaller the foreign source income and the lower the foreign tax credit limit. Although the affiliate rules generally exclude foreign corporations, a special provision applies to foreign affiliates that are 80% owned and where 50% of earnings are effectively connected to U.S. business to prevent firms from hiding their interest in these types of affiliates. If the effectively connected earnings are greater than 80%, all interest and assets are taken into account. If the effectively connected earnings are between 50% and 80%, only the effectively connected assets and earnings are included. This change provides that all assets and interest are included as long as effectively connected earnings are 50% or more. This proposal is estimated to raise $405 million over 10 years.

Repeal of 80/20 Rules

Under current law, dividends and interest paid by a domestic corporation are generally U.S. source income and subject to gross basis withholding if paid to a foreign person. (As discussed earlier in this report, portfolio interest and bank deposit interest paid to foreigners is exempt.) Interest and dividends paid by a firm with a least 80% of its gross income foreign source and due to an active foreign business are not subject to withholding. This interest can also increase foreign source income and the foreign tax credit limit. The determination of eligibility is made during the previous three-year period. The provision repeals the 80/20 company rules (and also the 80/20 rules for resident alien individuals). It grandfathers existing 80/20 companies if they also meet a new test (that combines the company with its existing subsidiaries) and if it does not add a new substantial line of business. It also excludes payment of interest on existing obligations. This provision is estimated to raise $153 million over 10 years.

Technical Correction to the HIRE Act

The provision makes a technical correction to the foreign compliance provisions of the Hiring Incentives to Restore Employment Act (P.L. 111-147) to clarify the statute of limitations.

SUMMARY OF LEGISLATIVE PROPOSALS

This section summarizes current legislative proposals that are designed to address or have consequences for international tax evasion and avoidance.

American Jobs and Closing Loopholes Act (H.R. 4213, 111th Congress)

As noted above, most foreign provisions in H.R. 4213 were included in the act, P.L. 111-226. Below are two provisions, one specifically a foreign provision and one related to foreign tax issues, that were not included.

Source Rules on Guarantees

Dividends and interest are generally sourced depending on the residence of the payor, whereas payments for services are sourced to the country where the service is performed. The treatment of guarantee fees is unclear, depending on whether compared to interest or services. Sourcing these payments like services allows U.S. subsidiaries of foreign firms to make deductible payments that reduce U.S. income without paying the withholding tax (as they would with interest). This provision treats these fees the same as interest: sourced to the residence of the payor. Payments by foreign persons are also U.S. source if allocable to income effectively connected with U.S. business. Treasury is to identify other transactions that are in the nature of guarantees. This proposal is estimated to raise $2.025 billion over 10 years.

Boot-Within-Gain Revisions

The boot-within-gain revisions are generally applicable to domestic as well as foreign activities but have implications for international transactions. When a person or firm sells stock and uses the proceeds to purchase other stocks, capital gain is recognized to the extent that the sales price of the stock exceeds the basis of that stock (typically what was originally paid for it). In general, a gain is not recognized in exchanges of stock in corporate reorganizations. If the exchange includes cash or property *(boot)*, gain is recognized to the extent of the boot. If the boot is more than the gain, all of the boot will not be taxed. However, if the boot is considered equivalent to a dividend, it will be taxed in full. One of the rules that allows the payment not to be considered as a dividend is a termination of interest (liquidation). Check-the-box rules permit a transaction to be considered a liquidation for U.S. purposes (i.e., a disregarded entity) but not for foreign purposes. Thus, one foreign subsidiary of a U.S. firm can pay cash to the U.S. parent for stock in another foreign subsidiary of the U.S. firm without the transactions being viewed as a dividend repatriation, thereby potentially reducing U.S. tax. In addition, two U.S. subsidiaries of a foreign parent can engage in a similar transaction without generating a U.S. withholding tax on the dividend. If the foreign parent does not have a treaty eliminating the tax, this treatment reduces U.S. taxes. This revision would treat payments in these cases as a dividend.

This provision was included in the President's budget proposals and estimated to raise $3.6 billion from FY2015 to FY2024.[127]

President Obama's International Tax Proposals[128]

President Obama's international proposals include several proposals that relate to multinational corporations: allocation of deductions and credits, a restriction on use of foreign tax credits when associated income is not recognized, and a restriction on check-the-box. They also include proposals addressing individual tax evasion. International provisions have been presented in each budget. One provision in the first (FY2010) budget ending check-the-box was dropped in subsequent budgets. Otherwise, provisions were continued and expanded over time. Overall, these provisions are projected to raise $276 billion for FY2015-FY2024 as presented in the current FY2015 budget. The provisions are discussed in the order in which they are presented unless otherwise noted, because revenue effects depend on that order. The budget also proposes additional resources for the IRS for international enforcement. In addition to budget proposals, President Obama presented a separate corporate tax reform proposal that included international provisions. This proposal included five elements: the allocation of interest for deferred income (discussed below), a tax on excess intangibles (discussed below), a minimum tax on foreign source income in low tax countries, disallowing a deduction for the cost of moving abroad, and providing a 20% credit for costs of moving an operation from abroad to the United States.[129]

Some of the President's proposals have been adopted. Two provisions relating to foreign tax credits were enacted in P.L. 111-226 (foreign tax credits and reverse hybrids, and the 80/20 rule). The HIRE Act (P.L. 111-147) included a provision treating equity swaps and other dividend equivalent payments as dividends; the other foreign compliance provisions were, in most cases, also in the President's. These provisions are not listed below.

The remainder of this section summarizes provisions in the President's budget proposals.

Provisions Affecting Multinational Corporations and Other Tax Law Changes

Hybrid Entities and Check-the-Box (FY2010 Budget Only)

The most significant provision in the FY2010 budget, based on revenue gain, is a revision directed at hybrid entities and check-the-box. This provision requires that a corporation cannot disregard a subsidiary corporation unless it is incorporated in the same jurisdiction. This rule does not apply to the parent and its first level subsidiary. Thus, a U.S. parent with a subsidiary in a low tax country could treat that subsidiary as a branch (disregard it as a separate entity). The subsidiary in the low-tax country, however, could not treat its own high-tax country subsidiary as a disregarded entity. This provision was included in the FY2010 proposals, where it was projected to raise $86.5 billion for FY2010-FY2019. It was not included in later budgets.

Allocation of Deductions and Credits

Two of these proposals would allocate deductions and credits, so as to deny those benefits until income is repatriated. This approach was included in a tax reform bill introduced by Chairman Rangel of the Ways and Means Committee in 2007 (H.R. 3970). A portion of overall deductions, such as interest, that reflect the share of foreign deferred income, would be disallowed until the income is repatriated. The foreign tax credit allocation rule would allow credits for the share of foreign taxes paid that is equal to the share of foreign source income repatriated, a provision the discussion of the proposals refers to as pooling. Disallowed deductions and credits would be carried forward. The proposal specifically excludes deductions for research and experimentation from the allocation rule. The FY2011 and subsequent budget proposals were narrower and limited to interest deductions; they also included a different set of allocation rules.

The revenue gain for FY2015-FY2024 was $43.2 billion for the limit on interest deductions and $74.6 billion for the foreign tax credit pooling.

Taxing Excess Returns on Intangibles

This provision, which did not appear in the 2010 budget proposal but appeared in subsequent budgets, would treat excess returns in a low-tax country on intangibles transferred to it from the United States as Subpart F income (subject to current taxation) and in a separate foreign tax credit basket (so that other foreign taxes could not offset U.S. taxes due on the excess returns). This provision is projected to raise $26.0 billion for FY2015-FY2024.

Transfer Pricing of Intangibles

The proposal would clarify several rules that are relevant to the transfer of intangibles. First, it would clarify that intangibles include workforce in place, goodwill, and going concern value. Second, it would allow the IRS commission to aggregate intangibles if that leads to a more appropriate value. Finally, it would clarify that intangibles are valued at their highest and best as it would be by a willing buyer and seller with reasonable knowledge of the relevant facts. This provision is projected to raise $2.7 billion for FY2015-FY2024.

Disallow Deductions for Reinsurance Premiums to Foreign Affiliates

U.S. insurance companies can reduce taxes by purchasing reinsurance from foreign affiliates, with a deduction of the premiums by the U.S. firm but no tax on the income of the foreign affiliate. This provision would disallow these deductions for reinsurance premiums when they are more than 50% of the basic premiums received. This provision was not in the FY2010 budget; it is projected to raise $7.5 billion in revenue for FY2015-FY2024.

Restrict Deductions for Excessive Interest of Members of Financial Reporting Groups

The proposal would allocate interest deductions among related firms that consolidate financial reporting, based on the share of earnings of each firm. This provision is projected to raise $48.6 billion for FY2015-FY2024.

Prevent Repatriation of Earnings in Cross-Border Transactions (Boot Within Gain)

The plan includes a proposal to require that distributions that are characterized as reorganizations but are in the nature of a dividend repatriation are subject to tax. This issue arises within the framework of an exchange of stock on the one hand for stock and property (called *boot*) and rules that provide the minimum of gain be based on the boot or overall gain. This proposal was projected to raise $297 million from FY2010 to FY2019. The 2011 budget includes a broader provision regarding to boot within gain that covers domestic transactions as well, and such a provision is also included in H.R. 4213.

Foreign Tax Credits for Dual-Capacity Taxpayers

This provision would restrict foreign tax credits for taxes paid where there is an income tax that is paid in part to receive a benefit (i.e., the firm is paying a tax in a dual capacity) to the amount that would be paid if the taxpayer were not a dual-capacity taxpayer. This provision typically relates to taxes being substituted for royalties in oil-producing countries; there is a provision that it will not abrogate any existing treaties. This provision was projected to raise $10.4 billion for FY2015-FY2024.

Tax Gain on the Sale of a Partnership Interest on Look-Through Basis

This provision, first appearing in the FY2013 budget outline, would require gain on sale of a partnership interest to be treated as income effectively connected to U.S. business (and thus taxable) to the extent of the transferor partner's effective connected income. It is projected to raise $2.8 billion for FY2015-FY2024.

Prevent Use of Leveraged Distributions from Foreign Related Corporations to Avoid Dividend Treatment

This provision, first appearing in the FY2013 budget outline, would address a mechanism to avoid treatment of a payment as a dividend (but rather a reduction in basis) when a foreign corporation funds the payment from a separate related foreign corporation. It is projected to raise $3.5 billion for FY2015-FY2024.

Extend Section 338(h)(16) to Certain Asset Acquisitions

This provision, first appearing in the FY2013 budget outline, extends rules limiting the ability of firms to increase foreign tax credits for certain asset acquisitions. It is projected to raise $1 billion for FY2015-FY2024.

Remove Foreign Taxes from a Section 902 Corporation's Foreign Tax Credit Pool When Earnings Are Eliminated

This provision first appears in the FY2013 budget outline. Current law allows a foreign tax credit for dividends paid or deemed paid or certain transactions. This provision reduces foreign tax credits for any action that reduces earnings and profits, since a reduction in earnings and profits will ultimately reduce the potential amount of dividends. It is projected to raise $0.4 billion for FY2015-FY2024.

Create a New Category of Subpart F Income for Transactions Involving Digital Goods or Services

The proposal would create a new category of Subpart F income, foreign base company digital income. It would include income of a controlled foreign company (CFC) from the lease or sale of a digital copyrighted article or from the provision of a digital service developed by a related party. It is projected to raise $11.7 billion for FY2015-FY2024.

Present Avoidance of Foreign Base Company Sales Income Through Manufacturing Service Arrangements

Among income included in Subpart F and subject to current taxation is foreign base company sales income, income from a purchase and resale by a related corporation of property manufactured outside the CFC's jurisdiction and sold outside that jurisdiction. This provision expands that treatment to property manufactured outside of, but on behalf of, the firm. This provision is projected to raise $24.6 billion from FY2015-FY2024.

Restrict the Use of Hybrid Arrangements That Create Stateless Income

The proposal would disallow deductions for interest and royalty payments made to related parties under hybrid arrangements in which the income is not taxed in the other jurisdiction. It is projected to raise $0.9 billion in FY2015-FY2024.

Limit the Application of Exceptions Under Subpart F for Certain Transactions That Use Reverse Hybrids to Create Stateless Income

Subpart F, which imposes tax on easily manipulated income, has a same-country exception so that it generally does not apply to payments between related firms organized in the same country under the presumption that there is a tax payment and deduction at the same tax rate. However, in the case of a foreign reverse hybrid, where the firm is viewed as a corporation by the United States but a partnership by the foreign country, the U.S. corporation is not seen as a distinct entity and not subject to tax. The proposal would provide that the exception to Subpart F not apply in these cases. This provision is projected to raise $1.3 billion for FY2025-FY2024.

Limit the Ability of Domestic Entities to Expatriate

This provision would allow U.S. firms that merge with other firms and establish a foreign headquarters (invert) to be treated as U.S. firms as long as the U.S. firm's shareholders retain more that 50% ownership (the current level is 80%). The proposal would also disallow inversions if the new firm has substantial business activities in the United States and is primarily managed and controlled in the United States. In addition, the proposal would extend the inversion rules now covering corporations and partnerships with a trade or business to all partnerships. This provision is projected to raise $17 billion for FY2015-FY2024.

Provisions Relating to Individual Tax Evasion, Not Enacted in the HIRE Act

The President's proposals included a number of provisions relating to individual evasion, including reporting of information, withholding, and various penalties. Overall these provisions were projected to raise revenues of $8.7 billion from FY2010 to FY2019 in the FY2010 budget and $5.4 billion from FY2011-FY2021 in the FY2011 budget. Most of these provisions, or some version of them, were adopted in the HIRE Act, including increased reporting on foreign accounts (withholding and information on U.S. beneficial owners). The remaining provisions are summarized below. These provisions were not in subsequent budgets.

Reporting on Transfers

U.S. persons' financial intermediaries and qualified intermediaries would be required to report financial transfers. U.S. persons and qualified intermediaries would be required to report the formation or establishment of a foreign entity. The floor is $10,000 in the FY2010 budget proposal, but $50,000 in the FY2011 proposal.

Additional Information Reported on Tax Returns: Lower Floor

The HIRE Act required individuals who are required to file an FBAR (Foreign Bank and Financial Account Reports) to report this information on the tax return if the amount in the account is $50,000 or more, a provision similar to the FY2011 budget proposal. The FY2010 proposal had a lower floor of $10,000.

Burden of Proof and Presumption Provisions

The FY2010 proposal contains a number of provisions that provide evidentiary presumptions (shifts in the burden of proof) in civil and administrative cases. If an individual has a foreign account it is presumed to be large enough to require filing an FBAR. If a person has an account of over $200,000 it is presumed that failure to file is willful (which opens the possibility of criminal as well as higher civil penalties). If a payment subject to withholding is made to a foreign person on an FDAP, the presumption is that that person is not eligible for withholding.

Statute of Limitation: No Floor

The statute of limitations for cross-border transactions is extended from three to six years with no floor in the FY2010 budget proposal; in the HIRE Act and the FY2011 budget, it applies to instances where more than $5,000 of income is omitted.

The Wyden-Gregg and Wyden-Coats Tax Reform Bills

Major revisions to corporate international tax rules are also included in S. 3018, a general tax reform act introduced by Senators Wyden and Gregg in the 111th Congress, and a similar bill, S. 727, introduced by Senators Wyden and Coats in the 112th Congress.[130] As part of revenue to finance a lower tax rate, this bill eliminates deferral of tax on foreign source income (taxes income currently) which should largely eliminate any benefits of profit shifting, since income would be taxed in any case. It also imposes a per country foreign tax credit limit.

Chairman Camp's Territorial Tax Proposal (Included in H.R. 1, 113th Congress) and Senator Enzi's Bill (S. 2091, 112th Congress)

These proposals would shift from the current system of deferral to a territorial tax, where no tax would be imposed on active dividends of foreign subsidiaries. Moving to a territorial tax increases the benefits for profit shifting to low-tax jurisdictions because there is never an issue of subsequent taxation, as is the case with deferral. The Camp proposal would combine a territorial tax with a lower corporate tax rate, whereas S. 2091 is a stand-alone territorial tax provision. Both contain provisions to limit the scope of profit shifting, although it is not clear how effective they would be.[131]

The Camp proposal would limit the amount of borrowing by the U.S. parent and impose one of three anti-base-erosion options, two directed at intangible income. Option A is similar to a proposal made by President Obama in his budget proposals that would tax excess earnings on intangibles (in excess of 150% of costs) in low-tax jurisdictions as Subpart F. The inclusion would be phased out between a 10% and a 15% rate. Option B would tax income that is subject to an effective foreign tax rate below 10% unless it qualifies for a home country exception. The home country exception applies when a firm conducts an active trade or business in the home country, has a fixed place of business, and serves the local market. Option C would tax all foreign income from intangibles (whether earnings by the foreign subsidiary or royalty payments) but allow a deduction for 40%, resulting in a tax rate of 15% at a 25% statutory tax rate. Option C was adopted for the final tax reform bill, H.R. 1, which also lowered the U.S. corporate tax rate to 25%.

S. 2091 does not have provisions restricting borrowing. Its anti-base-erosion provisions are a version of Option B in the Camp proposal along with a version of the first part of Option C would be included. Income in countries with tax rates of half or less than the U.S. rate (17.5%) would be subject to tax. However, operations that conduct an active business, with employees and officers that contribute substantially, would be excepted except to the extent the income is intangible income of the CFC. The CFC's intangible income would be Subpart F income. These rules provide more scope for exemption as compared to the rules in the Discussion Draft which would require exempt income to carry out activities serving the home country market. The bill also includes the first part of Option C, allowing a 17.5% tax rate on intangible income (such as royalties) earned by a domestic corporation. Intangible income would be placed in a separate foreign tax credit basket.

Stop Tax Haven Abuse Act[132]

This bill was introduced in the 111th Congress by Senator Carl Levin (S. 506) and by Representative Lloyd Doggett (H.R. 1265). Some of the provisions or related provisions in the bills were included in the HIRE Act. Provisions in the Stop Tax Haven Abuse that are addressed in the HIRE Act (P.L. 111-147) include burden of proof (Section 101), statute of limitations (Section 104), information reporting on U.S. beneficiaries of foreign accounts (Section 105), trust abuses (Section 106), treatment of dividend equivalents (Section 108), and passive foreign investment corporations (PFICs; Section 109). In addition, the health reform legislation, P.L. 111-148, included the economic substance doctrine. The original bill's provisions are summarized below, followed by summaries of bills from the 112th, 113th, and 114th Congresses.

111th Congress (S. 506 and H.R. 1245)

Section 101 would provide a burden of proof change. It would require the taxpayer involved in offshore secrecy jurisdictions to produce evidence, based on the presumption that the taxpayer is in control, that funds or other property are not taxable income, and that the account is not large enough to trigger a reporting threshold. (The bill also addresses securities law issues.) This section also contains the list of 34 tax haven jurisdictions taken from IRS court filings, and provides Treasury with the authority to add or remove jurisdictions. An important standard for being excluded from the list is an effective, and automatic, exchange of information.

Section 102 would expand the provisions in the Patriot Act of 2001, which gave Treasury the authority to require domestic financial institutions to take special measures (including providing information and prohibiting transactions) with respect to foreign jurisdictions relating to money laundering to cover instances of impeding U.S. tax enforcement.

Section 103 would require a publicly traded corporation or one with gross assets of $50 million or more whose management and control occurs primarily in the United States to be treated as a U.S. company. This provision is directed at shell corporations, including hedge funds and investment management businesses, set up in jurisdictions such as the Cayman Islands. It would not apply to subsidiaries of U.S. corporations simply because some decisions are made at the parent headquarters, but would still apply to shell subsidiaries.

Section 104 would extend the limit on audit periods from three years to six years for offshore jurisdictions with secrecy laws.

Section 105 would require U.S. financial institutions and brokers to file 1099 forms for any foreign account when they know the beneficial owner is a U.S. person. It would also require these institutions to report to the IRS when they set up offshore accounts and entities.

Section 106 addresses potential trust abuses. Foreign trusts have employed liaisons called trust protectors as a way for shielding U.S. taxpayers exercising control over the trust; the legislation provides that any powers held by a trust protector would be attributed to the trust grantor. It also provides that any U.S. person benefitting from a trust is treated as a beneficiary even if not named in the trust instrument, that future or contingent beneficiaries are treated as current ones, and that loans of assets and property as well as cash or security are treated as trust distributions.

Section 107 addresses legal opinions, stating that an activity is more likely than not to survive challenge by the IRS, which are used to shield taxpayers from large penalties. The legislation provides that a legal opinion of this nature would not apply in an offshore secrecy jurisdiction, providing exceptions to protect legitimate operations.

Section 108 would prevent dividend equivalents from escaping the dividend withholding tax.

Section 109 addresses reporting by PFICs by codifying proposed regulations regarding PFIC reporting by direct or indirect shareholders who are U.S. persons, and also requiring reporting by U.S. persons who directly or indirectly cause the PFIC to be formed or sent or receive assets.

Some of the sections of title II of the bill affect securities law rather than tax issues. Some provisions are tax-related, however.

Section 204 addresses an IRS John Doe summons where the IRS does not know the names of taxpayers and now must ask courts for permission to serve the summons. This section provides that in any case involving offshore secret accounts, the court is to presume tax compliance is at issue, to relieve the IRS of the obligation when the only records sought are U.S. bank records, and to allow them to issue John Doe summonses for large investigative projects without addressing each set of summonses separately.

Section 205 would address issues relating to the Foreign Bank and Financial Account Report (FBAR) requirement for a person controlling a foreign financial account of over $10,000. This is an additional rule from the requirement to report this information on the tax return, and IRS is now charged with enforcing this FBAR requirement. This provision would amend tax disclosure rules to more easily permit IRS to use tax data, change the penalty to refer to the highest average in the account during a year (and not on a specific day), and allow IRS access to information on Suspicious Activity Reports (SAR).

The last title of the bill relates to abusive tax shelters, and contains several provisions. It would strengthen penalties, prohibit the patenting of tax shelters, require development of an examination procedure so that bank regulators could detect questionable tax activities, disallow fees contingent on tax savings for tax shelters, remove communication barriers between enforcement agencies, codify regulations and make it clear that prohibition of disclosure by tax preparers does not prevent congressional subpoenas, and provide standards for tax shelter opinion letters. It would also codify the economic substance doctrine, to require both an objective and subjective test for economic substance.

112th Congress (S. 1346 and H.R. 2669)

Section 101 would extend the sanctions for money laundering to impeding tax enforcement (similar to previous provision in Section 102).

Section 102 would strengthen and clarify FATCA (Foreign Account Tax Compliance Act, adopted as part of the HIRE Act) in a variety of ways, including additional burden of proof requirements, expand the types of accounts that need to be disclosed, and other revisions.

Section 103 is similar to Section 103 in the previous bill.

Section 104 is similar to Section 105 of the previous bill.

Section 105 would require credit default swap (CDS) payments sent from the United States to be sourced as U.S. income and subject to tax.

Section 106 would treat funds deposited in U.S. accounts as U.S. source income subject to tax.

Some of the sections in the next title do not relate to taxes. Those that do include

Section 201 would require multinational corporations to provide the Securities and Exchange Commission (SEC) with country by country information.

Section 202 would provide a penalty up to $1 million for hiding offshore stock holdings.

Section 205 is similar to Section 204 in the previous bill.

Section 206 is similar to Section 205 in the previous bill.

The final title of the bill relates to abusive tax shelters and is similar to provisions in the previous legislation.

113th Congress (H.R. 1554, S. 1533, and H.R. 3666)

H.R. 1554, introduced by Representative Doggett, is similar to the Stop Tax Haven Abuse Act in the 112th Congress. S. 1533, introduced by Senator Levin, and H.R. 3666, introduced by Representatives DeLauro and Doggett, differ in some respects from H.R. 1554.

The first two major sections of these bills are the same as the previous bill (Sections 101-105) and Sections 201, 202, 205, and 206.

The final section of the bills, entitled "Ending Corporate Offshore Tax Avoidance," contains substantive changes in the treatment of multinationals, similar to some of those that have been included in the President's proposals (discussed above). They include the allocation of expenses and foreign tax credit pooling, treatment of income from intangibles to low-taxed affiliates as Subpart F income, limitations on income shifting through intangible property transfers, a repeal of check-the-box rules for certain foreign entities and CFC look-through rules, and allocations of interest deductions.

114th Congress

Representative Doggett and Senator Whitehouse announced introduction of a Stop Tax Haven Abuse Act in January 2014. The bill is similar to S. 1533 and H.R. 3666, although the interest allocation is broader and an additional section introduces the changes in treatment of inversions in the President's budget (such as treating any merger with a foreign firm in which U.S. shareholders maintain majority interests as a U.S. firm).[133]

Finance Committee Proposal, 111th Congress

A draft of this proposal was circulated on March 12, 2009, and has been discussed by Sullivan.[134] Several of its proposals were included in the HIRE Act (statute of limitations, requiring FBAR information to be filed with the tax return, increasing trust penalties to a minimum of $10,000, expanding the definition of distributions, and increasing the penalties for underpayments associated with foreign accounts).

- It would require entities transferring funds offshore to report to the IRS the amount, destination, and account information. Publicly traded companies would be excluded.

- The statute of limitations would be extended from three to six years for tax returns that report or should have reported certain international transactions.
- It would require the foreign bank and financial account report (FBAR) to be filed with the tax returns.
- Tax preparers would be required to ask due diligence questions to determine whether an FBAR should be filed.
- The foreign trust failure-to-file penalty would be increased to a $10,000 minimum and the definition of property considered to be a distribution for foreign trusts would be expanded, and would include artwork and jewelry.
- Fines and penalties on payments attributable to certain offshore transactions would be doubled.
- A provision in the Heroes Earnings Assistance and Relief Tax Act of 2008 (P.L. 110-245) would be modified to require offshore entities that hire workers under a government contract be treated as American employers by establishing a rule that any individual who performs at least 100 hours of service a month is an employee and not an independent contractor.

Fraud Enforcement and Recovery Act, S. 386, 111th Congress

This proposal, introduced by Chairman Leahy of the Senate Judiciary Committee, included a provision to apply the international money laundering statute to tax evasion, and set aside funds for the Justice Department to pursue financial fraud, including funds to the tax division. It had been passed by the Senate. The House version of the bill, H.R. 1748, and the enacted law, P.L. 111-21, did not include the tax provision but did include additional funds.

Incorporation Transparency and Law Enforcement Assistance Act, S. 1483, H.R. 3416, 112th Congress

This proposal (introduced as S. 569 in the 111th Congress) would establish uniform requirements for states relating to the disclosure of beneficial owners of corporations and limited liability companies, including updating and maintenance of information after terminating, imposing additional requirements for those not U.S. citizens or permanent residents, providing penalties, and updating of such disclosures. It also authorizes a study of requirements of partnerships, trusts, and other legal entities. This bill is relevant, among other things, to issues raised about the use of states as international tax havens.

Additional Proposals in the 113th Congress

A number of bills introduced in the 113th Congress would have made a variety of changes in the tax law affecting the treatment of foreign source income. H.R. 694 (Representative Schakowsky) and S. 250 (Senator Sanders) would have made fundamental changes similar in some respects to the Wyden-Coats bill: treat firms managed and controlled in the United States as domestic firms, repeal deferral, impose a per country foreign tax credit limit, and limit credits for dual capacity tax payers. H.R. 3793 (Representative Maffei) and S. 1844 (Senator Shaheen) would adopt the management and control provision. H.R. 1555 (Representative Doggett) also would adopt this provision, as well as repeal the look-through rule for royalties and certain intangible income and adopt the boot-within-gain provision discussed above. After the problem of firms inverting via merger became prominent, bills that incorporated the President's proposal to treat as domestic firms mergers with U.S. firms and other provisions included H.R. 4679 (Representative Levin), S. 2360 (Senator Levin), H.R. 4985 (Representative Van Hollen), and S. 2489 (Senator Walsh). H.R. 5338 also included the management and control provision, and S. 2489 also included allocation of income provisions. S. 268 (Senator Levin) is a bill that includes many of the provisions of the various Stop Tax Havens Abuse legislation but not the fundamental law changes of the Sanders bill (S. 250).

End Notes

1 See U.S. Senate Subcommittee on Investigations, *Staff Report on Dividend Tax Abuse*, September 11, 2008.

2 Joseph Guttentag and Reuven Avi-Yonah, "Closing the International Tax Gap, In Max B. Sawicky, ed. *Bridging the Tax Gap: Addressing the Crisis in Federal Tax Administration*, Washington, DC, Economic Policy Institute, 2005. Most recently, Gabriel Zucman estimated a revenue loss of $36 billion for evasion of tax on financial investments. See Gabriel Zucman, Taxing Across Borders: Tracing Personal Wealth and Corporate Profits, *Journal of Economic Perspectives*, Vol. 28, no. 4, Fall, 2014, pp, 121-148.

3 The Foreign Account Tax Compliance Act was enacted in 2010 as part of the Hiring Incentives to Restore Employment Act (P.L. 111-147). See CRS Report R43444, *Reporting Foreign*

Financial Assets Under Titles 26 and 31: FATCA and FBAR, by Erika K. Lunder and Carol A. Pettit.

[4] Most recently, Zucman estimated, using two different methodologies, $54 billion and $133 billion for 2013. Gabriel Zucman, Taxing Across Borders: Tracing Personal Wealth and Corporate Profits, *Journal of Economic Perspectives*, Vol. 28, no. 4, Fall, 2014, pp, 121-148.

[5] See "Obama Backs Corporate Tax Cut If Won't Raise Deficit," *Bloomberg*, January 25, 2011, http://www.bloomberg.com/news/2011-01-26/obama-backs-cut-in-u-s-corporate-tax-rate-only-if-it-won-t-affect- deficit.html.

[6] See CRS Report R42624, *Moving to a Territorial Income Tax: Options and Challenges*, by Jane G. Gravelle, for a discussion of the Camp and Enzi proposals.

[7] For a chronology of earlier years, see Martin Sullivan, "Proposals to Fight Offshore Tax Evasion, Part 3," *Tax Notes* May 4, 2009, p. 517.

[8] In the 113th Congress, H.R. 1554, H.R. 3666, and S. 1533 were introduced. In the 112th Congress, a revised version of the Stop Tax Haven Abuse Act (H.R. 2669 and S. 1346) was introduced. In addition to these bills, in the 111th Congress, a different bill, S. 386, introduced by Chairman Leahy of the Senate Judiciary Committee, would have expanded the money-laundering provisions to include tax evasion and provided additional funding for the tax division of the Justice Department. S. 569, also introduced by Chairman Levin, would have imposed requirements on the states for determination of beneficial owners of corporations formed under their laws. This proposal has implications for the potential use of incorporation in certain states as a part of an international tax haven plan. Other bills addressing international issues have also been introduced.

[9] Memo on Offshore Profit Shifting and the U.S. Tax Code, at http://www.levin.senate.gov/newsroom/press/release/subcommittee-hearing-to-examine-billions-of-dollars-in-us-tax-avoidance-by-multinational-corporations/?section= alltypes.

[10] Organization for Economic Development and Cooperation, *Harmful Tax Competition: An Emerging Global Issue*, 1998, p. 23.

[11] J.R. Hines and E.M. Rice, "Fiscal Paradise: Foreign Tax havens and American Business," *Quarterly Journal of Economics*, vol. 109, February 1994, pp. 149-182.

[12] Government Accountability Office, International Taxation: Large U.S. Corporations and Federal Contractors with Subsidiaries in Jurisdictions Listed as Tax Havens or Financial Privacy Jurisdictions, GAO-op-157, December 2008.

[13] J. C. Sharman, *Havens in a Storm, The Struggle for Global Tax Regulation*, Cornell University Press, Ithaca, New York, 2006; Martin A. Sullivan, "Lessons From the Last War on Tax Havens," *Tax Notes*, July 30, 2007, pp. 327-337.

[14] David Spencer and J.C. Sharman, International Tax Cooperation, *Journal of International Taxation*, published in three parts in December 2007, pp. 35-49, January 2008, pp. 27-44, 64, February 2008, pp. 39-58.

[15] For a discussion of these cases see Joint Committee on Taxation *Tax Compliance and Enforcement Issues With Respect to Offshore Entities and Accounts*, JCX-23-09, March 30, 2009. The discussion of UBS begins on p. 31 and the discussion of LGT begins on p. 40. This document also discusses the inquiries of the Permanent Subcommittee on Investigations of the Senate Homeland Security Committee relating to these cases.

[16] Anthony Faiola and Mary Jordan, "Tax-Haven Blacklist Stirs Nations: After G-20 Issues mandate, Many Rush to Get Off Roll," *Washington Post*, April 4, 2009, p. A7.

[17] This announcement by the Organization for Economic Development and Co-operation (OECD) was posted at http://www.oecd.org/document/0/0,3343,en_2649_34487_ 42521280_1_1_1_1,00.html.

[18] David D. Stewart, "G-20 Declares End to Bank Secrecy as OECD Issues Tiered List," *Tax Notes*, April 6, 2009, pp.38-39.

[19] Organization for Economic Development and Cooperation, http://www.oecd. org/dataoecd/50/0/43606256.pdf.

[20] OECD, Global Forum on Transparency and Exchange of Information for Tax Purposes, Tax Transparency: 2014 Report on Progress, http://www.oecd.org/tax/transparency /GFannualreport2014.pdf.

[21] See, for example, Micheil van Dijk, Francix Weyzig, and Richard Murphy, *The Netherlands: A Tax Haven*? SOMO (Centre for Research on Multinational Corporations), Amsterdam, 2007 and Rosanne Altshuler and Harry Grubert, "Governments and Multinational Corporations in the Race to the Bottom, Tax Notes, February 27, 2009, pp. 979-992.

[22] Fergal O'Brien, "Bono, Preacher on Poverty, Tarnishes Halo Irish Tax Move," October 15, 2006, Bloomberg.com, http://bloomberg.com/apps/news?pid=20601109&refer= home&sid =aef6sR60oDgM#.

[23] See Jesse Drucker, "Google 2.4% Rate Shows How $60 Billion Lost to Tax Loopholes," *Bloomberg,* October 21, 2010, posted at http://www.bloomberg.com/news/2010-10-21/google-2-4-rate-shows-how-60-billion-u-s-revenue-lost- to-tax-loopholes.html and "Yahoo, Dell Swell Netherlands' $13 Trillion Tax Haven," *Bloomberg,* January 23, 2013, posted at http://www.bloomberg.com/news/2013-01-23/yahoo-dell-swell-netherlands-13-trillion-tax-haven.html.

[24] In 2013, the Dutch government adopted a motion to stop the use of arrangements in the Netherlands. See Accountancy Live, Dutch Sandwich Tax Loophole Looks Likely to be Closed, April 12, 2013, https://www.accountancylive.com/dutch-sandwich-tax-loophole-looks-set-be-closed. According to information received from the Embassy of the Netherlands, the Netherlands has adopted unilateral measures, including exchange of information with treaty partners regarding legal entities incorporated in the Netherlands which lack economic substance that are engaged in financial transactions.

[25] EY Tax Insights, "European Union, Ireland, Luxembourg and Netherlands: State Aid – Commission Investigates Transfer Pricing Arrangements on Corporate Taxation of Apple (Ireland), Starbucks (Netherlands) and Fiat Finance and Trade (Luxembourg)," Ernst and Young, June 2014, http://taxinsights.ey.com/archive/archive-news/european- union—ireland—luxembourg-and-netherlands—state-aid—commission.aspx. A further inquiry in Luxembourg regarding Amazon was opened in October, 2014, and a general inquiry of all member states was initiated in December 2014. See European Commission, State aid: Commission Extends Information Enquiry on Tax Rulings Practice to all Member States, December 17, 2014, at http://europa.eu/rapid/press-release_IP-14-2742_en.htm.

[26] Council of the European Union, Parent-Subsidiary Directive: Council Agrees to Add Anti-Abuse Clause Against Corporate Tax Avoidance, December 9, 2014, http://www.consilium. europa.eu/uedocs/cms_data/docs/pressdata/en/ ecofin/146127.pdf.

[27] Charles Gnaedinger, "Luxembourg P.M Calls out U.S. States as Tax Havens" *Tax Notes International*, April 6, 2009, p. 13.

[28] See http://www.offshore-fox.com/offshore-corporations/offshore_corporations_0401.html.

[29] Another offshore website lists in addition to the countries in Table 1 Austria, Campione d'Italia, Denmark, Hungary, Iceland, Madeira, Russian Federation, United Kingdom, Brunei, Dubai, Lebanon, Canada, Puerto Rico, South Africa, New Zealand, Labuan, Uruguay, and the United States. See http://www.mydeltaquest.com/english/.

[30] See http://www.offshore-manual.com/taxhavens/.

[31] "Haven Hypocrisy," *The Economist*, March 26, 2008.

[32] Michael McIntyre, "A Program for International Tax Reform," *Tax Notes*, February 23, 2009, pp. 1021-1026.

[33] Charles Gnaedinger, "U.S., Cayman Islands Debate Tax Haven Status," *Tax Notes*, May 4, 2009, p. 548-545.

[34] The City of London is the small, 1.22 square mile area at the center of the larger city of London. It contains the financial district.

[35] Nicholas Shaxson, *Treasure Islands: Uncovering the Damage of Offshore Bankers and Tax Havens*, Palgrave MacMillan, New York, 2011.

[36] Anthony van Fossen, *Tax Havens and Sovereignty in the Pacific Islands*, St. Lucia, Queensland, Australia, University of Queensland Press, 2012.

[37] See http://www.oecd.org/document/60/0,3343,en_2649_34897_1942460_1_1_1_1,00.html.

[38] For tax rates see http://www.worldwide-tax.com/index.asp#partthree.

[39] Tax Justice Network, *Tax Us if You Can*, September, 2005.

[40] Ronen Palan, Richard Murphy, and Christian Chavagneux, *Tax Havens: How Globalization Really Works*, Ithaca, Cornell University Press, 2012.

[41] Effects on economic activity are addressed in CRS Report RL34115, *Reform of U.S. International Taxation: Alternatives*, by Jane G. Gravelle.

[42] Harry Grubert, "Intangible Income, Intercompany Transactions, Income Shifting and the Choice of Locations," *National Tax Journal*, vol. 56, March 2003, Part II, pp. 221-242.

[43] Simon J. Pak and John S. Zdanowicz, U.S. Trade With the World, An Estimate of 2001 Lost *U.S. Federal Income Tax Revenues Due to Over-Invoiced Imports and Under-Invoiced Exports*, October 31, 2002.

[44] CRS Report R40178, *Tax Cuts on Repatriation Earnings as Economic Stimulus: An Economic Analysis*, by Donald J. Marples and Jane G. Gravelle.

[45] In 2004 the interest allocation rules were changed to allocate worldwide interest, but the implementation of that provision was delayed and has not yet taken place. See CRS Report RL34494, *The Foreign Tax Credit's Interest Allocation Rules*, by Jane G. Gravelle and Donald J. Marples.

[46] See CRS Report RL34249, *The Tax Reduction and Reform Act of 2007: An Overview*, by Jane G. Gravelle.

[47] U.S. Department of Treasury, *Report to Congress on Earnings Stripping, Transfer Pricing and U.S. Income Tax Treaties*, November 2007.

[48] See CRS Report R43568, *Corporate Expatriation, Inversions, and Mergers: Tax Issues*, by Donald J. Marples and Jane G. Gravelle for a discussion.

[49] The Treasury Department issued new proposed regulations relating to cost sharing arrangements. See Treasury Decision 9441, Federal Register, vol. 74, No. 2, January 5, 2009, pp. 340-39, http://www.transferpricing.com/pdf/ TD_9441.pdf. These rules include a periodic adjustment which would, among other aspects, examine outcomes. See "Cost Sharing Periodic Payments Not Automatic, Officials Say," *Tax Notes*, February 23, 2009, p. 955.

[50] Michael McDonald, "Income Shifting from Transfer Pricing: Further Evidence from Tax Return Data," U.S. Department of the Treasury, Office of Tax Analysis, OTA Technical Working Paper 2, July 2008.

[51] Jesse Drucker, "Google 2.4% Rate Shows How $60 Billion Lost to Tax Loopholes," *Bloomberg,* October 21, 2010, posted at http://www.bloomberg.com/news/2010-10-21/google-2-4-rate-shows-how-60-billion-u-s-revenue-lost-to-tax- loopholes.html, and "Yahoo, Dell Swell Netherlands' $13 Trillion Tax Haven," *Bloomberg,* January 23, 2013, posted at http://www.bloomberg.com/news/2013-01-23/yahoo-dell-swell-netherlands-13-trillion-tax-haven.html.

[52] Editorial Board, "Ireland, Still Addicted to Tax Breaks," *New York Times*, October 20, 2014, http://www.nytimes.com/2014/10/20/opinion/ireland-still-addicted-to-tax-breaks.html?_r=0.

[53] Szu Ping Chang, "Facebook Hid £440m in Cayman Islands Tax Haven," The Telegraph, December 23, 2012, at http://www.telegraph.co.uk/finance/newsbysector/banksandfinance/9763615/Facebook-hid-440m-in-Cayman-Islands- tax-haven.html; Lori Hinnant, "Europe Takes On Tech Giants And Tax Havens," *Associated Press*, at http://www.manufacturing.net/news/2012/12/europe-takes-on-tech-giants-and-tax-havens.

[54] See for example William W. Chip, "'Manufacturing' Foreign Base Company Sales Income," *Tax Notes*, November 19, 2007, p. 803-808.

[55] See David R. Sicular, "The New Look-Through Rule: W(h)ither Subpart F? *Tax Notes*, April 23, 2007, pp. 349-378 for a discussion of the look-through rules under Section 954(c)(6).

[56] For a discussion of reverse hybrids see Joseph M. Calianno and J. Michael Cornett, "Guardian Revision: Proposed Regulations Attach Guardian and Reverse Hybrids," *Tax Notes International*, October 2006, pp. 305-316.

[57] See Sean Foley, "U.S. Outbound: Cross border Hybrid Instrument Transactions to gain Increased Scrutiny During IRS Audit," http://www.internationaltaxreview.com/?Page=10&PUBID=35&ISS=24101&SID=692834&TYPE=20. Andrei Kraymal, International Hybrid Instruments: Jurisdiction Dependent Characterization, *Houston Business and Tax Law Journal*, 2005, http://www.hbtlj.org/v05/v05Krahmalar.pdf.

[58] Government Accountability Office, U.S. Multinational Corporations: Effective Tax Rates are Correlated With Where Income is Reported, GAO-08-950, August 2008. Melissa Costa and Jennifer Gravelle, "Taxing Multinational Corporations: Average Tax Rates," *Tax Law Review*, vol. 65, no. 3, spring 2012, pp. 391-414; Jennifer Gravelle, Who Will Benefit from a Territorial Tax, Presented at the 105th Conference of the National Tax Association, 2012.

[59] Harry Grubert, "Tax Credits, Source Rules, Trade and electronic Commerce: Behavioral Margins and the Design of International Tax Systems. *Tax Law Review*, vol. 58, January 2005; also issued as a CESIFO Working Paper no. 1366, December 2004; Harry Grubert and Rosanne Altshuler, "Corporate Taxes in a World Economy: Reforming the Taxation of Cross-Border Income," in John W. Diamond and George Zodrow, eds., Fundamental Tax Reform: Issues, Choices and Implications, Cambridge, MIT Press, 2008.

[60] Data on earnings and profits of controlled foreign corporations are taken from Lee Mahoney and Randy Miller, Controlled Foreign Corporations 2004, Internal Revenue Service *Statistics of Income Bulletin*, Summer 2008, http://www.irs.ustreas.gov/pub/irs-soi/04coconfor.pdf. Data on gross domestic product (GDP) from Central Intelligence Agency, *The World Factbook*, https://www.cia.gov/library/publications/the-world-factbook.Data for profits for 2008 and 2010 multinational earnings from U.S. Statistics of Income, U.S. Corporations and Their Controlled Foreign Corporations, http://www.irs.gov/uac/SOI-Tax-Stats-Controlled-Foreign-Corporations. Data on GDP from Central Intelligence Agency, *The World Factbook*, https://www.cia.gov/ library/ publications/ the-world-factbook. Most GDP data to compare with the 2004 earnings is from 2008 and based on the exchange rate, but for some countries only earlier years and data based on purchasing power parity were available. GDP data to compare with 2010 earnings were from 2013 data. These data are those posted on the website at the time the ratios were calculated. Because GDP data are from somewhat later years, the ratios may be slightly understated.

[61] These ratios changed between 2004 and 2010. For 2004, the remaining G-7 countries accounted for 38% of rest-of- world GDP and 32% of earnings, the countries in **Table 3** accounted for 5% of rest-of-world GDP and 30% of earnings, and the countries in **Table 4** accounted for less than 1% of rest-of-world GDP and 14% of earnings.

[62] One offshore website points out that Canada can be desirable as a place to establish a holding company; see Shelter Offshore, http://www.shelteroffshore.com/index.php/offshore/more/canada_offshore.

[63] Harry Grubert and Rosanne Altshuler, "Corporate Taxes in a World Economy: Reforming the Taxation of Cross- Border Income," in John W. Diamond and George Zodrow, eds., *Fundamental Tax Reform: Issues, Choices and Implications, Cambridge*, MIT Press, 2008.

[64] Government Accountability Office, *U.S. Multinational Corporations: Effective Tax Rates are Correlated With Where Income is Reported*, GAO-08-950, August 2008.

[65] Melissa Costa and Jennifer Gravelle, "U.S. Multinationals Business Activity: Effective Tax Rate and Location Decisions, National Tax Association Proceedings from the 103rd Annual Conference, 2010; http://www.ntanet.org/ images/stories/pdf/proceedings/10/13.pdf.

[66] Martin Sullivan, U.S. Citizens Hide Hundreds of Billions in the Caymans, *Tax Notes*, May 24, 2004, p. 96.

[67] Martin Sullivan, "Extraordinary Profitability in Low-Tax Countries," Tax Notes, August 25, 2008, pp. 724-727. Note that the effective tax rates for some countries differ considerably

depending on the source of data; the Netherlands would be classified as a low tax country based on data controlled foreign corporations but high tax based on BEA data. See Government Accountability Office, *U.S. Multinational Corporations: Effective Tax Rates are Correlated With Where Income is Reported*, GAO-08-950, August 2008.

[68] See James R. Hines, Jr., "Lessons from Behavioral Responses to International Taxation," National Tax Journal, vol. 52 (June 1999): 305-322, and Joint Committee on Taxation, *Economic Efficiency and Structural Analyses of Alternative U.S. Tax Policies for Foreign Direct Investment*, JCX-55-08, June 25, 2008, for reviews. Studies are also discussed in U.S. Department of Treasury, *The Deferral of Income of Earned Through Controlled Foreign Corporation*, May, 2000, http://www.treas.gov/offices/tax-policy/library/subpartf.pdf.

[69] This point is made by The Treasury Inspector General for Tax Administration, "A Combination of Legislative Actions and Increased IRS Capability and Capacity are Required to Reduce the Multi-billion Dollar U.S. International Tax Gap," January 27 2009, 2009-I-R001.

[70] This discussion focuses on the consequences for U.S. revenues, but profit shifting also affects revenues in other countries. For a review of the literature and issues, see International Monetary Fund, Spillovers in International Corporate Taxation, May 9. 2014, http://www.imf.org/external/np/pp/eng/2014/050914.pdf.

[71] U.S. Department of the Treasury, IRS, Report on the Application and Administration of Section 482, 1999.

[72] Joint Committee on Taxation, *Estimates of Federal Tax Expenditures for 2014-2018*, October 31, 2008, JCX-97-14, August 5, 2014, https://www.jct.gov/publications. html?func=startdown&id=4663.

[73] Budget for FY2015, *Analytical Perspectives*, p. 210. http://www.whitehouse.gov /sites/default/files/omb/budget/fy2015/assets/spec.pdf.

[74] Harry Grubert and Rosanne Altshuler, "Corporate Taxes in *the World Economy," in Fundamental Tax Reform: Issues, Choices, and Implications* ed. John W. Diamond and George R. Zodrow, Cambridge, MIT Press, 2008.

[75] For historical and projected revenues, see Congressional Budget Office, http://www.cbo.gov/publication/45010, 2014.

[76] "Shifting Profits Offshore Costs U.S. Treasury $10 Billion or More," Tax Notes, September 27, 2004, pp. 1477-1481; "U.S. Multinationals Shifting Profits Out of the United States," Tax Notes, March 10, 2008, pp. 1078-1082. $75 billion in profits is artificially shifted abroad. If all of that income were subject to U.S. tax, it would result in a gain of $26 billion for 2004. Sullivan acknowledges that there are many difficulties in determining the revenue gain. Some of this income might already be taxed under Subpart F, some might be absorbed by excess foreign tax credits, and the effective tax rate may be lower than the statutory rate. Sullivan concludes that an estimate of between $10 billion and $20 billion is appropriate. Altshuler and Grubert suggest that Sullivan's methodology may involve some double counting; however, their own analysis finds that multinationals saved $7 billion more between 1997 and 2002 due to check-the-box rules. Some of this gain may have been at the cost of high-tax host countries rather than the United States, however. See Rosanne Altshuler and Harry Grubert, "Governments and Multinational Corporations in the Race to the Bottom," *Tax Notes International*, February 2006, pp. 459-474.

[77] Martin Sullivan, "Transfer Pricing Costs U.S. At Least $28 Billion," *Tax Notes*, March 22, 2010, pp. 1439-1443.

[78] Charles W. Christian and Thomas D. Schultz, ROA-Based Estimates of Income Shifting by Multinational Corporations, *IRS Research Bulletin*, 2005 http://www.irs.gov/pub/irs-soi/05christian.pdf.

[79] Simon J. Pak and John S. Zdanowicz, U.S. Trade With the World, An Estimate of 2001 Lost *U.S. Federal Income Tax Revenues Due to Over-Invoiced Imports and Under-Invoiced Exports*, October 31, 2002.

[80] Kimberly Clausing, Multinational Firm Tax Avoidance and Tax Policy, *National Tax Journal*, vol. 62, December 2009, pp. 703-725, Working Paper, March 2008. Her method involved estimating the profit differentials as a function of tax rate differentials over the period 1982-2004 and then applying that coefficient to current earnings.

[81] Kimberly A. Clausing and Reuven S. Avi-Yonah, *Reforming Corporate Taxation in a Global Economy: A Proposal to Adopt Formulary Apportionment*, Brookings Institution: The Hamilton Project, Discussion paper 2007-2008, June 2007.

[82] Douglas Shackelford and Joel Slemrod, "The Revenue Consequences of Using Formula apportionment to Calculate U.S. and Foreign Source Income: A Firm Level Analysis," *International Tax and Public Finance*, vol. 5, no. 1, 1998, pp. 41-57.

[83] Kimberly A. Clausing, "The Revenue Effects of Multinational Firm Income Shifting," *Tax Notes*, March 28, 2011, pp. 1580-1586.

[84] Gabriel Zucman, "Taxing Across Borders: Tracing Personal Wealth and Corporate Profits", *Journal of Economic Perspectives*, vol. 28, no. 4, Fall, 2014, pp, 121-148.

[85] These studies are discussed and new research presented in U.S. Department of Treasury, *Report to Congress on Earnings Stripping, Transfer Pricing and U.S. Income Tax Treaties*, November 2007. One study used a different approach, examining taxes of firms before and after acquisition by foreign versus domestic acquirers, but the problem of comparison remains and the sample was very small; that study found no differences. See Jennifer L. Blouin, Julie H. Collins, and Douglas A. Shackelford, "Does Acquisition by Non-U.S. Shareholders Cause U.S. firms to Pay Less Tax?" *Journal of the American Taxation Association*, Spring 2008, pp. 25-38. Harry Grubert, *Debt and the Profitability of Foreign Controlled Domestic Corporations in the United States*, Office of Tax Analysis Technical Working Paper No. 1, July 2008, http://www.ustreas.gov/offices/tax-policy/library/otapapers/otatech2008.shtml#2008.

[86] In addition to the 2007 Treasury study cited above, see Jim A. Seida and William F. Wempe, "Effective Tax Rate Changes and Earnings Stripping Following Corporate Inversion," *National Tax Journal*, vol. 57, December 2007, pp. 805-828. They estimated $0.7 billion of revenue loss from four firms that inverted. Inverted firms may, however, behave differently from foreign firms with U.S. subsidiaries.

[87] Harry Grubert, "Intangible Income, Intercompany Transactions, Income Shifting, and the Choice of Location," *National Tax Journal*, Vo. 56,March 2003, Part 2.

[88] Rosanne Altshuler and Harry Grubert, "Governments and Multinational Corporations in the Race to the Bottom," *Tax Notes International*, February 2006, pp. 459-474.

[89] Data are presented in "Who's Watching our Back Door?" *Business Accents*, Florida International University, Fall 2004, pp. 26-29.

[90] Jost H. Heckemeyer and Michael Overesch, Multinationals' Profit Response to Tax Differentials: Effect Size and Shifting Channels, Center for European Economic Research, Discussion Paper 13-045, 2013, http://ftp.zew.de/pub/ zew-docs/dp/dp13045.pdf.

[91] Data are taken from Melissa Redmiles, "The One-Time Dividends-Received Deduction," Internal Revenue Service *Statistics of Income Bulletin*, spring 2008, http://www.irs.ustreas.gov/pub/irs-soi/08codivdeductbul.pdf.

[92] Rodney P. Mock and Andreas Simon, "Permanently Reinvested Earnings: Priceless," *Tax Notes*, November 17, 2008, pp. 835-848.

[93] See CRS Report R43444, *Reporting Foreign Financial Assets Under Titles 26 and 31: FATCA and FBAR*, by Erika K. Lunder and Carol A. Pettit.

[94] OECD, Multilateral Competent Authority Agreement, October 29, 2014, http://www.oecd.org/tax/exchange-of-tax- information/multilateral-competent-authority-agreement.htm.

[95] See Joint Committee on *Taxation Tax Compliance and Enforcement Issues With Respect to Offshore Entities and Accounts*, JCX-23-09, March 30, 2009, p. 6 for a discussion.

[96] This history is described by Reuven Avi-Yonah in testimony before the Committee on Select Revenue Measures of the Ways and Means Committee, March 5, 2008.

[97] Joseph Guttentag and Reuven Avi-Yonah, "Closing the International Tax Gap," in Max B. Sawicky, ed. *Bridging the Tax Gap: Addressing the Crisis in Federal Tax Administration*, Washington, D.C., Economic Policy Institute, 2005.

[98] Testimony of Reuven Avi-Yonah, Subcommittee on Select Revenue Measures, Ways and Means Committee, March 31, 2009.

[99] "Brown Pushes U.K. Tax havens On OECD Standards" *Tax Notes International*, April 20, 2009, pp. 180-181.

[100] A very clear and brief explanation of the origin of the QI program and of the requirements can be found in Martin Sullivan, "Proposals to Fight Offshore Tax Evasion," *Tax Notes*, April 20, 2009, pp. 264-268.

[101] For additional discussion of the QI program, see Joint Committee on Taxation, *Tax Compliance and Enforcement Issues With Respect to Offshore Entities and Accounts*, JCX-23-09, March 30, 2009.

[102] Martin A. Sullivan, "Proposals to Fight Offshore Tax Evasion," *Tax Notes*, April 20, 2009.

[103] Joseph Guttentag and Reuven Avi-Yonah, "Closing the International Tax Gap," in Max B. Sawicky, ed. *Bridging the Tax Gap: Addressing the Crisis in Federal Tax Administration*, Washington, D.C., Economic Policy Institute, 2005.

[104] Tax Justice Network, *Tax Us If You Can*, September, 2005.

[105] Tax Justice Network, *Estimating the Price of Offshore*, July22, 2012, at http://www.taxjustice.net/cms/front_content.php?idcat=148.

[106] Gabriel Zucman, "Taxing Across Borders: Tracing Personal Wealth and Corporate Profits," *Journal of Economic Perspectives*, vol. 28, no. 4, Fall, 2014, pp, 121-148.

[107] See OECD, "Action Plan on Base Erosion and Profit Shifting," http://www.oecd.org/ ctp/BEPSActionPlan.pdf.

[108] CRS Report RL34115, *Reform of U.S. International Taxation: Alternatives*, by Jane G. Gravelle.

[109] Firms with 80% continuity of ownership would be treated as U.S. firms and firms with at least 60% continuity of ownership would be subject to tax on the transfer of assets for the next 10 years.

[110] See CRS Report RL34115, *Reform of U.S. International Taxation: Alternatives*, by Jane G. Gravelle. See also International Corporate Tax Reform Proposals: Issues and Proposals, Forthcoming, *Florida Tax Review*, by Jane G. Gravelle.

[111] Senate Finance Committee, "Baucus Unveils Proposals for International Tax Reform," November 19, 2013, at http://www.finance.senate.gov/newsroom/chairman/release/?id=f946a9f3-d296-42ad-bae4-bcf451b34b14.

[112] *The President's Framework for Business Tax Reform: A Joint Report by the White House and the Department of the Treasury*, February 2012, http://www.treasury.gov/resource-center/tax-policy/Documents/The-Presidents-Framework- for-Business-Tax-Reform-02-22-2012.pdf

[113] Douglas Shackelford and Joel Slemrod, "The Revenue Consequences of Using Formula apportionment to Calculate U.S. and Foreign Source Income: A Firm Level Analysis," *International Tax and Public Finance*, vol. 5, no. 1, 1998, pp. 41-57.

[114] Kimberly A. Clausing and Reuven A. Avi-Yonah, *Reforming Corporate Taxation in a Global Economy : A Proposal to Adopt Formulary Apportionment*, Brookings Institution: The Hamilton Project, Discussion paper 2007-08, June 2007.

[115] These and other issues are discussed by Rosanne Altshuler and Harry Grubert, "Formula Apportionment: Is it Better than the Current System and Are There Better Alternatives?" *National Tax Journal*, vol. 63, no. 4, pt. 2, December 2010, pp. 1145-1184.

[116] Ibid.

[117] See European Commission, 'European Corporate Tax Base: Making Business Easier and Cheaper," press release, March 16, 2011, http://europa.eu/rapid/press-release_IP-11-319_en.htm?locale=en

118 Michael P. Devereux and Simon Loretz, "The Effects of EU formula Apportionment on Corporate Tax Revenues," *Fiscal Studies*, Vol. 29, no. 1, March 2008, pp. 1-33. http://www3.interscience.wiley.com/cgi-bin/fulltext/119399105/PDFSTART?CRETRY=1&SRETRY=0.

119 Michael McIntyre, "A Program for International Tax Reform," *Tax Notes*, February 23, 2009, pp. 1021-1026.

120 See Department of the Treasury, *General Explanations of the Administration's Fiscal Year 2015 Revenue Proposals*, March 2014, http://www.treasury.gov/resource-center/tax-policy/Documents/General-Explanations- FY2015.pdf.

121 Harry Grubert, "Tax Credits, Source Rules, Trade and Electronic Commerce: Behavioral Margins and the Design of International Tax Systems," Tax Law Review, vol. 58, January 2005; also issued as CESIFO Working Paper no. 1366, December 2004.; Harry Grubert and Rosanne Altshuler, "Corporate Taxes in a World Economy: Reforming the Taxation of Cross-Border Income," in John W. Diamond and George Zodrow, eds., *Fundamental Tax Reform: Issues, Choices and Implications, Cambridge*, MIT Press, 2008.

122 For discussions of various proposals listed see Tax Justice Network, "Ending the Offshore Secrecy System," March 2009, http://www.taxjustice.net/cms/upload/pdf/TJN_0903_Action_Plan_for_G-20.pdf ; testimony of Reuven Avi- Yonah, Peter Blessing, Stephen Shay, and Douglas Shulman before the Subcommittee on Select Revenue Measures of the Ways and Means Committee, March 31, 2009; Martin Sullivan, "Proposals to Fight Offshore Tax Evasion," *Tax Notes*, part 1, April 20, 2009, pp. 264-268; part 2: April 27, 2009, pp. 371-373; part 3, May 4, 2009, pp. 516-520; Reuven Avi-Yonah, Testimony before the Committee on Select Revenue Measures of the Ways and Means Committee, March 5, 2008; Testimony of Jack A. Blum and, Testimony on the Cayman Islands and Offshore Tax Issues before the Senate finance Committee, July 24, 2008; Michael McIntyre, "A Program for International Tax Reform," *Tax Notes*, February 23, 2009, pp. 1021-1026.

123 See Jeremiah Coder, "Proposed offshore Crime Legislation Worries Defense Bar," *Tax Notes Today*, March 23, 2009. The attorneys are concerned that money laundering charges would not have to be approved through the Department of Justice's tax division, that penalties of up to 20 years gives prosecutors too much power, that the provisions may trap taxpayers who want to participate in IRS voluntary disclosure, and that they would also discourage the "quiet disclosure" where taxpayers simply report past information.

124 P.L. 111-226 has no short title.

125 Press release at http://waysandmeans.house.gov/press/PRArticle.aspx?NewsID=11191; summary at http://waysandmeans.house.gov/media/pdf/111/America_Jobs_Summary.pdf.

126 Revenue estimates for H.R. 4213 are in JCX-30-10, May 28, 2010. https://www.jct.gov/publications.html?func= startdown&id=3685.

127 See Treasury Greenbooks, at http://www.treasury.gov/resource-center/tax-policy/Pages/general_explanation.aspx.

128 These proposals are listed in the various Treasury Greenbooks, at http://www.treasury.gov/resource-center/tax- policy/Pages/general_explanation.aspx.

129 *The President's Framework for Business Tax Reform: A Joint Report by the White House and the Department of the Treasury*, February 2012, http://www.treasury.gov/resource-center/tax-policy/Documents/The-Presidents-Framework- for-Business-Tax-Reform-02-22-2012.pdf.

130 See "Obama Backs Corporate Tax Cut If Won't Raise Deficit," *Bloomberg*, January 25, 2011, http://www.bloomberg.com/news/2011-01-26/obama-backs-cut-in-u-s-corporate-tax-rate-only-if-it-won-t-affect- deficit.html.

131 See CRS Report R42624, *Moving to a Territorial Income Tax: Options and Challenges, by Jane G. Gravelle*, for additional discussion.

132 For a more detailed explanation of the 111th Congress bill, see Senator Levin's Introductory Remarks, March 3, 2009. This proposal has also been discussed by Martin Sullivan, "Proposals to Fight Offshore Tax Evasion, Part 3," *Tax Notes*, May 4, 2009, pp. 516-520.

For a discussion of the 112th Congress bill see Senator Levin's Introductory Remarks, July 12, 2011.

133For a summary of the bill, see http://doggett.house.gov/images/ doggettstoptaxhavenabuseactsummary.pdf.

134 See Committee on Finance News Release, March 12, 2009, http://finance.senate.gov/press/Bpress/2009press/prb031209b.pdf; See also Martin A. Sullivan, "Proposals to fight Offshore Tax Evasion, Part 2," Tax Notes, April 27, 2009, pp. 371-373.

In: Corporate Profit Shifting
Editor: Dorian L. Peters
ISBN: 978-1-63483-767-5

Chapter 3

U.S. INTERNATIONAL CORPORATE TAXATION: BASIC CONCEPTS AND POLICY ISSUES*

Mark P. Keightley and Jeffrey M. Stupak

INTRODUCTION

Recent deficit reduction and tax reform plans have included broad proposals to reform the U.S. international corporate tax system. These proposals have raised concerns over how changing the way American multi-national corporations are taxed could impact the deficit and debt, domestic job markets, competitiveness, and the use of corporate tax havens, among other things. An informed debate about how to reform the system governing the taxation of U.S. multi-national corporations requires careful consideration of these issues, as well as a basic understanding of several features of the current system.

This report provides a general introduction to the basic concepts and issues relevant to the U.S. international corporate tax system. The explanations provided in this report emphasize the underlying concepts of the international tax system and are intended to be as simplified as possible. There are of course

* This is an edited, reformatted and augmented version of a Congressional Research Service publication R41852 , prepared for Members and Committees of Congress, dated December 2, 2014.

important and complex technical details that would need to be considered carefully if reform of the current system were to be implemented effectively and efficiently. These important technical details, however, are beyond the scope of this report.

WORLDWIDE VERSUS TERRITORIAL TAXATION

The United States taxes American corporations on their worldwide income.[1] This approach to taxation is referred to as a worldwide (or resident-based) tax system. Examples of other countries that take this general approach include Chile, Ireland, Mexico, and South Korea. The most commonly used alternative to the worldwide tax system is known as a territorial (or source-based) system. If the U.S. were to employ a territorial tax system, it would tax American corporations only on the income they earned within the physical borders of the United States. Countries that have adopted a territorial type system include Australia, Austria, Belgium, Canada, the Czech Republic, Denmark, Finland, France, Germany, Greece, Italy, Japan, the Netherlands, Norway, Portugal, Spain, Sweden, Switzerland, Turkey, and the United Kingdom, among others.[2]

In reality, no country has either a pure worldwide or a pure territorial tax system. In a pure worldwide tax system a country would allow domestic corporations to claim a full credit for foreign taxes paid, although no country allows this. In a pure territorial tax system a country would completely forgo taxing any of the income earned abroad by domestically based corporations; however, every country taxes some amount of corporate income earned abroad. Pure forms of either system would likely limit the ability to address abusive tax evasion practices and would result in other countries changing their tax systems for their own benefit.[3] Thus, in practice the distinction between having a "worldwide" or "territorial" tax system is generally one of degree.

Still, the pure-form systems each have an important property that serves as a point of departure in the international tax reform debate. A pure worldwide tax system exhibits what is known as "capital export neutrality," which states that taxes should be irrelevant to a corporation's decisions to invest at home or overseas (i.e., export capital). Wherever a corporation locates their investment (production facility, manufacturing plant, etc.), they face the same tax on the resulting income. In theory, this should lead corporations to allocate their capital to its most productive use in the *world* economy. In addition, global economic output (income) will be maximized if all other countries use a worldwide system since foreign corporations will similarly allocate their capital to its most productive use in the world economy.

A pure territorial system exhibits what is known as "competitive neutrality," also known as "capital import neutrality." With a pure territorial system, corporations making overseas investments face the same tax rates as foreign competitors in foreign markets. This, in theory, should remove any tax-based competitive disadvantage of corporations in foreign markets. For example, consider an American car maker and a Japanese car maker, both with production facilities in Japan. With a territorial system, the two car makers would both pay the same in total taxes on the income earned in Japan. The American and Japanese car makers would be competitively neutral with respect to taxes as a result. This system is not neutral in an economic sense, however, because it causes more investment in low-tax countries than would occur without taxes.

A third concept of "neutrality" that is often referenced in the worldwide versus territorial debate is known as "national neutrality." National neutrality corresponds to a worldwide tax system with a deduction for foreign taxes paid instead of a full tax credit. Allowing a deduction instead of a credit decreases the after-tax return to investing abroad relative to investing at home and results in more domestic investment and corporate income than with a pure worldwide system. Additionally, a deduction is less costly to the government than a credit, so government tax revenues are higher. As a result, total national income is maximized assuming foreign countries do not change their tax rules in response.

DEFERRAL, SUBPART F INCOME, AND ACTIVE FINANCING

While the U.S. has a worldwide-based tax system, current law allows American corporations with foreign subsidiaries to defer paying taxes on income earned abroad until that income is repatriated (returned) to the United States.[4] This represents a benefit to American corporations, which, all else equal, prefer to pay taxes later rather than sooner. In the extreme, deferral could allow an American corporation to completely avoid U.S. taxation if they never repatriate their overseas income. The income earned by foreign branches of American corporations, however, is not deferrable.[5]

A particular type of income which does not qualify for deferral is "subpart F income." Named for the location in the Internal Revenue Code where its tax treatment is defined, subpart F income generally includes passive types of income such as interest, dividends, annuities, rents, and royalties.[6] The highly fungible nature of subpart F income is such that corporations can use overseas subsidiaries to transfer taxable income from high-tax countries to low-tax countries with the ultimate goal of reducing their U.S. income tax liability. To prevent this, corporations must pay taxes on subpart F income in the year it is generated, regardless of whether it is actually repatriated to the United States.[7]

An important exception to the subpart F income tax rules exists for "active financing income." The active financing exception relates to the income earned by American corporations that operate banking, financing, and insurance lines of business abroad. Although some of the income derived from these lines of business (e.g., interest, dividends, and annuities) could be labeled as passive, they are excepted from subpart F if the income was generated as a result of active business operations. On the one hand, there is the argument that there are real economic rationale for keeping this income abroad and that transactions involving active financing income are not necessarily for tax avoidance purposes. On the other hand, it could be argued that passive income is passive income, regardless of the underlying line of business. Nonetheless, active financing income qualifies for deferral and is only taxed when it is repatriated to the United States.

THE FOREIGN TAX CREDIT

When American corporations repatriate income from subsidiaries operating abroad, that income may have already been taxed by a foreign country. If it has, corporations are generally allowed to claim a dollar-for-dollar tax credit (up to a limit) for foreign taxes paid. The credit, formally known as the foreign tax credit, is intended to alleviate the double taxation of corporate income.[8] The credit is generally limited to the amount of taxes a corporation would pay in the credit's absence, which is effectively just the U.S. corporate tax rate multiplied by the amount of income earned abroad. In other words, an American corporation may claim the foreign tax credit up to the point that the credit reduces its U.S. tax on foreign-earned income to zero, but no further. Additionally, a separate credit must be calculated for two types of income "baskets"—passive and non-passive income.

As long as the U.S. corporate tax rate is higher than the foreign county's rate, the foreign tax credit should—in principle—result in the corporation owing the same amount in total taxes (U.S. plus foreign) as it would if it earned the income in the Unites States. When the foreign tax rate is higher than the U.S. tax rate, a corporation will end up paying total world taxes (U.S. plus foreign) at the higher foreign rate. Additionally, in such a circumstance the corporation could end up with "excess" foreign credits because of the limits that restrict the credit from reducing U.S. taxes owed below zero.

An example may help in understanding the mechanics of the foreign tax credit. Consider an American corporation that pays taxes in the U.S. at the top corporate rate of 35%, and that has a subsidiary located in a country with a 25% tax rate. If the corporation earned $100 of income abroad, it would pay $25 in foreign taxes. When the corporation repatriates this income it would initially owe $35 in U.S. taxes. Before actually paying this tax, however, the corporation could claim a foreign tax credit of $25, reducing its U.S. tax liability from $35 to $10. Notice that this corporation pays a total of $35 in taxes worldwide, corresponding to a 35% world tax rate on foreign earned income.

The example above assumes that the foreign tax rate is lower than the U.S. tax rate, which need not be the case. Consider the case were the foreign tax rate is 45% instead of 25%. The corporation would pay $45 in foreign taxes on the $100 of income earned abroad. When the corporation repatriates this income it would still initially owe the U.S. $35 in taxes. This time, however, the corporation's available $45 in foreign tax credits exceeds its U.S. taxes owed. As a result, the corporation could use its $45 in foreign tax credit to reduce its $35 U.S. tax liability to zero, leaving it with $10 in "excess" credits. Notice that this corporation pays a total of $45 in taxes worldwide, corresponding to a 45% world tax rate on foreign earned income. The next section discusses how firms can use excess credits from one country to offset earnings from another country.

Cross-Crediting

Cross-crediting refers to American corporations applying excess foreign tax credits generated in a high-tax country to U.S. tax owed on income generated in a low-tax country. This is possible because deferral allows corporations to selectively decide when to repatriate income and therefore when to use excess credits.

Mechanics of Cross-Crediting

	Low-Tax Subsidiary	High-Tax Subsidiary
Earnings:	$100	$100
Foreign taxes paid:	$10	$45
U.S. taxes owed:	$35	$35
U.S. taxes after credit:	25	-$10
U.S. taxes paid:	$15	

By choosing to repatriate income from low-tax countries when excess foreign tax credits exist, corporations can lower the amount of U.S. tax they would otherwise have to pay. In essence, this practice allows corporations to use tax credits related to one source of income (from high-tax countries) to offset taxes on unrelated income (from low-tax countries). This could be argued to go against the relief of double taxation objective of the foreign tax credit. Corporations, however, are not allowed to use excess credits associated with passive income to offset taxes on active income, or vice versa.

To understand the basic mechanics of cross-crediting consider another example. Suppose an American corporation has two foreign subsidiaries, each earning $100. One subsidiary is located in a low-tax country and pays $10 in foreign taxes (10% tax rate), and the other is located in a high-tax country and pays $45 in foreign taxes (45% tax rate). When the corporation repatriates the foreign-earned income of its subsidiaries it will initially owe $35 in U.S. taxes for each one (35% tax rate). The corporation can apply the high-tax country subsidiary's $45 foreign tax credit to that subsidiary's $35 U.S. tax liability, leaving it with $10 in excess credits. The corporation can then apply the low-tax country subsidiary's $10 foreign tax credit to that subsidiary's $35 U.S. tax liability, leaving it with $25 in U.S. taxes still due. Finally, the corporation can cross-credit the $10 in excess credits from the high-tax subsidiary and reduce the low-tax subsidiary's final U.S. tax liability from $25 to $15. The result is the corporation pays less in U.S. taxes than if cross-crediting were prohibited.

PROFIT SHIFTING

Profit shifting generally refers to corporations artificially moving taxable income from high-tax countries to low-tax countries as part of a tax reduction strategy. A popular method used to accomplish this is debt shifting. By financing operations in high-tax countries with debt and financing operations in low-tax countries with equity (e.g., stock), corporations are able to deduct interest in countries where the deduction is most valuable and have income taxed in countries with the lowest rates. At the same time, the overall capital structure of the corporation (its mix of debt and equity) may remain the same indicating the financing strategy was tax motivated. Debt shifting can also involve the use of intercompany loans made between different parts of the company located in high-tax and low-tax countries. The ultimate goal is to claim interest deductions in high-tax countries and pay income in low-tax countries.[9] What are known as "thin" capitalization rules have been enacted in the U.S. and abroad to limit this strategy, but it continues to be utilized.

Another popular method used to shift profits involves intracompany transfers of intangible assets and intellectual property such as patents, copyrights, trademarks, trade secrets, etc. For example, an American corporation may form a subsidiary in a low-tax country and then sell the rights to use an intangible asset to it. A subsidiary of the same American corporation, but located in a high-tax jurisdiction, may then lease the right to use the intangible asset from the low-tax subsidiary. In exchange, the high-tax subsidiary would pay the low-tax subsidiary a royalty payment, perhaps at a markup. The royalty payment would reduce the taxable income of the high-tax subsidiary and simultaneously shift profits to the low-tax subsidiary.

A third strategy favored by corporations to shift profits involves charging prices that do not reflect market, or "arm's length," prices for goods transferred between subsidiaries. For example, a subsidiary in a low-tax country could overcharge a subsidiary in a high-tax country for a particular product. This would allow the high-tax subsidiary to claim a higher than normal deduction for the payments to the low-tax subsidiary, while also allowing the low-tax subsidiary to realize the payments as income. The U.S. and other countries have established what are known as transfer pricing rules that are intended to insure that transactions between related subsidiaries occur at market prices. Difficulty arises, however, when no clear market price exists, for example, with something such as intangible property.

Often times multiple tax planning strategies, such as the ones described above, are used in conjunction to minimize taxes. Several layers of subsidiaries operating in multiple countries may also be involved. Additionally, instead of these transactions occurring just between subsidiaries, they may occur between the U.S. parent corporation and a foreign subsidiary. The explanations provided here are for simplicity and it should be noted that analyzing and understanding the specific tax strategy used by a particular company can be extremely complex.[10]

BASE EROSION AND PROFIT SHIFTING (BEPS) ACTION PLAN

Growing concern at home and abroad over the methods used by multinational corporations—both U.S. and foreign—to avoid or delay paying taxes has led to calls for a coordinated effort to reduce profit shifting. As a result, the Organisation for Economic Co-operation and Development (OECD) has initiated development of an Action Plan on Base Erosion and Profit Shifting (BEPS) at the request of the G20 Finance Ministers.

The goal of the BEPS project is to develop 15 detailed actions governments can take to reduce tax avoidance by multinational corporations (as well as individuals) worldwide. The Action Plan is scheduled to be completed in three phases: September 2014, September 2015, and December 2015. Some of the actions will require coordination and information sharing between governments, and potentially the amendment of existing tax treaties. As a result, the Action Plan relies heavily on the participation of all major economies. A number of G20 countries that are not part of the OECD (Argentina, Brazil, China, India, Indonesia, Russia, Saudi Arabia, and South Africa) participated in the meetings that led to the eventual adoption of the Action Plan by all G20 finance ministers.

The OECD has been careful to stress that many of the strategies used by multinational corporations are likely legal. One reason corporations can move profits from high-tax to low-tax countries is the antiquated designs of international tax regimes. Current tax systems were not designed to handle highly mobile intellectual property and intangible assets. Patents, trademarks, and algorithms can be easily moved from one country to another with little or no change in real economic activity, taking with them the income they generate. Additionally, differences and lack of coordination between nations' tax systems can provide opportunities for companies to engage in tax minimization strategies. Lastly, there are various items in countries' tax codes and regulations that provide preferential tax treatment to certain income earned abroad, or that provide the opportunity for legal maneuvering. Some of these items were the result of intentional policy choices, others were not.

Making Tax Rate Comparisons

One of the main focal points in the debate over corporate tax reform is whether the top U.S. federal corporate tax rate of 35% is too high relative to the rest of the world.[11] This often referenced rate is the top *statutory* federal tax rate, defined as the legally imposed rate on taxable income. In many countries, including the U.S., non-federal governments (e.g., states) also levy a corporate income tax, which increases the total statutory rate corporations face. Regardless, because of a number of tax subsidies (deductions, credits, exemptions, etc.) in the corporate tax system, corporations' *effective* (or actual) tax rate is typically less than the statutory rate. The U.S. is not alone in having effective rates that differ from statutory rates. It is therefore more appropriate to look at total effective tax rates when comparing the U.S. to the rest of the world.[12]

It is also important to keep in mind that effective rates can vary substantially among U.S. corporations and across corporations in the same industry, complicating a general U.S. to rest-ofthe-world comparison. For example, some corporations rely more on debt financing, which is tax preferred to equity financing, reducing their effective tax rate. Some corporations and industries rely more on machines and facilities that can be depreciated ("written-off") more quickly than assets in others industries, which again leads to differing effective tax rates. Other corporations and industries have more extensive overseas operations, which affects their effective U.S. tax rate. In the end, an American corporation or an entire domestic industry could face higher or lower (or the same) effective tax rate as a foreign competitor—there is no one single effective tax rate that applies to all American corporations.

Finally, when making comparisons between U.S. and worldwide tax rates it is important to indicate whether tax rates are simple (unweighted) averages or whether they are adjusted (weighted) to account for the size of the economies being compared. If the U.S. tax rate is compared to world tax rates that are not weighted, then a small economy, such as Iceland, can have the same effect on the average international rate as a large economy, such as Germany or Japan. It is therefore more appropriate to compare the U.S. tax rate to an weighted average of international tax rates. Typically, each country's tax rate is weighted by its gross domestic product (GDP) when computing the average.

COMPETITIONVERSUS TRADE

A common argument that is made for lowering corporate tax rates or moving to a territorial tax system is that doing so will allow the U.S. to remain competitive in the global economy. It is important, however, to distinguish between competition and trade. American companies compete against each other and foreign counterparts for customers, market share, investors and the like. If one company does better, it is at the expense of the others in the industry. Thus, competition implies a contest, with winners and losers. In contrast, countries do not compete against each other, they trade with each other. When countries specialize in what they have a comparative advantage at producing and trade for what they have a comparative disadvantage at producing they are able to produce more together than in isolation. Greater production leads to more product variety, lower consumer prices, and greater average incomes.[13]

Although economists generally believe that trade leads to greater overall income, it is also recognized that particular groups may be hurt in the short-term as the economy shifts its specialization focus. There are a range of policy options available to Congress to assist those displaced by trade including subsidies to assist affected industries, unemployment insurance, and retraining programs, among others. The relevant issue when contemplating potential policy options is how to effectively target assistance to those hurt by trade while not preventing the recognition of the widespread benefits of trade.

SUMMARY AND RELATED READINGS

This report has provided an introduction to the U.S. international tax system. Understanding this basic foundation should help policymakers better understand and begin to evaluate many of the nuanced international tax issues. Going forward, questions to consider may include the following: Does the system need to be reformed in order for U.S. corporations to remain competitive? How far can the U.S. lower rates without negatively impacting the deficit? Are there any unintended consequences policymakers should be aware of when debating corporate tax reform?

End Notes

[1] The concepts discussed are described and analyzed in greater detail in CRS Report RL34115, *Reform of U.S. International Taxation: Alternatives*, by Jane G. Gravelle.

[2] Categorization of worldwide versus territorial type system was based on Ernst & Young, *Briefing: Corporate income tax (CIT) rates*, 2014, http://www.ey.com/GL/en/Services/Tax/Tax-policy-and-controversy/TPC-Briefing—Corporateincome-tax—CIT—rates, and Pricewaterhouse Coopers, *Evolution of Territorial Tax Systems in the OECD*, April 2, 2013, p. 3, http://www.techceocouncil.org/ clientuploads/reports/Report %20on %20 Territorial% 20Tax%20Systems_ 20130402b.pdf. There are some discrepancies between these two sources. For example, Poland is categorized by PWC as having a territorial system, but as having a worldwide system by E&Y. The converse is true for Israel. Aside from Ireland, which was only categorized by PWC, only those countries that were consistently categorized across both sources were included here. Also see U.S. Congress, Joint Committee on Taxation, *Background And Selected Issues Related To The U.S. International Tax System And Systems That Exempt Foreign Business Income*, 112th Cong., 1st sess., May 20, 2011, JCX-33-11 for more detail on other country's territorial based systems.

[3] There is an important legal distinction between tax avoidance and tax evasion. Tax avoidance refers to the use of all legal tax practices to lower ones tax liability. Tax evasion refers to illegal tax practices to lower ones tax liability.

[4] Repatriation is technically accomplished via a dividend payment from a foreign subsidiary to its American parent corporation.

[5] A foreign subsidiary is a legal entity separate from its parent company, while a foreign branch is an extension of a domestic company.

[6] Specifically, the tax treatment of subpart F income may be found in Sections 951 to 956 of the IRC.

[7] A rule called "check-the-box" has undermined subpart F provisions by allowing foreign subsidiaries to make transactions between themselves, such as loans and royalty payments, which are not recognized as taxable transactions by law. With check-the-box a corporation can set up a foreign subsidiary that owns another a foreign subsidiary. The company then "checks a box" on an IRS form choosing to have the lower level subsidiary treated as a disregarded (fiscally transparent) company for tax purposes. Transactions between the two subsidiaries are then treated as if they are occurring within the same company, avoiding the subpart F anti-deferral rules.

[8] Sections 901 to 909 of the IRC define the foreign tax credit rules.

[9] For a more detailed deduction of profit shifting and tax havens, see CRS Report R40623, *Tax Havens: International Tax Avoidance and Evasion*, by Jane G. Gravelle.

[10] For a specific example, see Edward D. Kleinbard, "Through a Latte Darkly: Starbuck's Stateless Income Planning," *Tax Notes*, June 24, 2013, pp. 1515-1535.

[11] For information on comparing corporate tax rates across countries, see CRS Report R41743, *International Corporate Tax Rate Comparisons and Policy Implications*, by Jane G. Gravelle.

[12] Technically, the “marginal effective tax rate” is the appropriate measure to look at. The marginal rate is the effective tax on a prospective investment. For more information see, CRS Report R41743, *International Corporate Tax Rate Comparisons and Policy Implications*, by Jane G. Gravelle.

[13] British economist David Ricardo first formalized the idea of comparative advantage in his 1817 book titled *On the Principles of Political Economy and Taxation*.

In: Corporate Profit Shifting
Editor: Dorian L. Peters
ISBN: 978-1-63483-767-5

Chapter 4

Reform of U.S. International Taxation: Alternatives*

Jane G. Gravelle

Summary

A striking feature of the modern U.S. economy is its growing openness—its increased integration with the rest of the world. The attention of tax policy makers has recently been focused on the growing participation of U.S. firms in the international economy and the increased pressure that engagement places on the U.S. system for taxing overseas business. Is the current U.S. system for taxing U.S. international business the appropriate one for the modern era of globalized business operations, or should its basic structure be reformed?

The current U.S. system for taxing international business is a hybrid. In part, the system is based on a residence principle, applying U.S. taxes on a worldwide basis to U.S. firms while granting foreign tax credits to alleviate double taxation. The system, however, also permits U.S. firms to defer foreign-source income indefinitely—a feature that approaches a territorial tax jurisdiction. In keeping with its mixed structure, the system produces a patchwork of economic effects that depend on the location of foreign investment and the circumstances of the firm. Broadly, the system poses a tax incentive to invest in countries with low tax rates of their own

* This is an edited, reformatted and augmented version of a Congressional Research Service publication RL34115, prepared for Members and Committees of Congress, dated June 3, 2015.

and a disincentive to invest in high-tax countries. In theory, U.S. investment should be skewed toward low-tax countries and away from high-tax locations.

Evaluations of the current tax system vary, and so do prescriptions for reform. According to traditional economic analysis, world economic welfare is maximized by a system that applies the same tax burden to prospective (marginal) foreign and domestic investment so that taxes do not distort investment decisions. Such a system possesses *capital export neutrality*, and could be accomplished by worldwide taxation applied to all foreign operations along with an unlimited foreign tax credit. In contrast, a system that maximizes national welfare—a system possessing *national neutrality*—would impose a higher tax burden on foreign investment, thus permitting an overall disincentive for foreign investment. Such a system would impose worldwide taxation but would permit only a deduction, and not a credit, for foreign taxes.

A tax system based on territorial taxation would exempt overseas business investment from U.S. tax. In recent years, several proponents of territorial taxation have argued that changes in the world economy have rendered traditional prescriptions for international taxation obsolete and instead prescribe territorial taxation as a means of maximizing both world and national economic welfare. For such a system to be neutral, however, capital would have to be completely immobile across locations. A case might be made that such a system is less distorting than the current hybrid system, but it is not clear that it is more likely to achieve policy goals than other reforms, including not only a movement toward worldwide taxation by ending deferral but also proposals to provide a minimum tax and restrict deductions for costs associated with deferred income or restrict deferral and foreign tax credits for tax havens.

INTRODUCTION

The increasingly global scope of U.S. business has a variety of dimensions. In trade, the overall level of exports plus imports has risen steadily and substantially in recent decades, increasing from 16% of U.S. gross domestic product (GDP) in 1976 to 30% of GDP in 2013. Cross-border investment is growing even more dramatically. In 1976, the ratio of U.S. private assets abroad to GDP was 0.20; by year-end 2013 the ratio was 1.39.[1]

The bulk of the increase in *outbound* investment has been portfolio investment—investment in financial assets such as stocks and bonds without the active conduct of overseas business operations. But foreign direct investment by U.S. firms—actual foreign production by U.S.- owned companies—has increased too, rising from a ratio of 0.12 of GDP to 0.42 of GDP between 1976 and 2013. It is the taxation of U.S. business operations that has been the recent focus of policy makers and that has raised the question of basic tax reform in the international sector: Is the current U.S. system for taxing U.S. international business appropriate in this age of globalized business operations, or is reform needed?[2] Moreover, along with the increasing scope of international investment activities, there is a growing opportunity for tax shelters that take advantage of low-tax foreign jurisdictions. How might revisions in the tax system exacerbate or address these tax shelter issues?

The current U.S. system is a hybrid construct, embodying a mix of opposing jurisdictional principles. Not surprisingly, the mixed system—in conjunction with foreign host-country taxes— poses a patchwork of incentive effects for U.S. firms and their global operations, in some cases taxing foreign operations favorably and creating an incentive to invest abroad, and in other cases imposing high tax burdens and posing a disincentive to overseas investment. In still other cases, the system presents a rough tax neutrality toward overseas investment. It is perhaps the hybrid nature of the system that has led to calls for reform. Prescriptions for a "good" tax system vary, and the hybrid system satisfies none of them fully.

This report describes and assesses the principal prescriptions that have been offered for broad reform of the international system. It begins with an overview of current law and possible revisions. It then sets the framework for considering economic efficiency as well as tax shelter activities. Finally, it reviews alternative approaches to revision in light of those issues.

THE CURRENT SYSTEM AND POSSIBLE REVISIONS

The System's Structure

There are two alternative, conceptually "pure," principles on which countries base their tax in the international setting: residence and territory. Under a residence system, a country taxes its own residents (or domestically chartered *resident* corporations) on their worldwide income, regardless of that income's geographic source. Under a territorial or source-based system, a country taxes only income that is earned within its own borders.

In practice, no country uses a pure residence-based tax; historically, virtually all countries tax income foreign investors earn within their borders (although they may grant tax holidays in some cases as an inducement to investment). Many countries, however, have a territorial or source-based tax (although they may tax some foreign-source income under anti-abuse rules).[3] The United States uses a system that taxes both income of foreign firms earned within its borders and the worldwide income of U.S.-chartered firms.

Despite these nominal residence features, however, U.S. taxes do not apply to the foreign income of U.S.-owned corporations chartered abroad. As a result, a U.S. firm can indefinitely defer U.S. tax on its foreign income if it conducts its foreign operations through a foreign-chartered subsidiary corporation; U.S. taxes do not apply as long as the foreign subsidiary's income is reinvested overseas. With some exceptions, U.S. taxes apply only when the income is remitted to the U.S.-resident parent as dividends or other intra-firm payments such as interest and royalties. The deferral feature reduces the effective U.S. tax burden on foreign income and imparts an element of territoriality to the system. It also results in a dichotomous structure for taxing overseas business income: deferral in the case of foreign-subsidiary income and current taxation in the case of branches of U.S. chartered corporations. The bulk of active business investment by U.S. firms is through foreign-chartered subsidiaries.[4]

Along with deferral, another basic feature of the U.S. system is the foreign tax credit. The United States taxes worldwide income on either a current or deferred basis, but it also allows credits for foreign taxes paid on a dollar-for-dollar basis against U.S. taxes otherwise owed.[5] This treatment avoids the double taxation that would otherwise apply and concedes the first right of taxation to the country of source. In effect, the United States gives the foreign host country the first opportunity to tax the income and collects only what tax is left (up to its own rate) after the foreign host country collects its share.

When the foreign tax is higher than the U.S. tax, the credit is limited to the U.S. tax that would be due on the foreign income. The purpose of the limit is to protect the U.S. domestic tax base— without it, foreign countries could impose very high taxes without discouraging inbound U.S. investment because the cost of the higher taxes would be shifted to the U.S. Treasury. With the limitation, if foreign taxes exceed the U.S. tax that would be due, the excess foreign taxes cannot be credited. Foreign tax credits that exceed this limitation are termed *excess credits*. Currently, foreign tax credits are allowed on what is sometimes termed an *overall* basis, so that income and tax credits from all countries are combined. This treatment allows for *cross-crediting*, in which credits paid in excess of U.S. tax in one country may be used to offset U.S. tax in a country in which the foreign tax is lower than the U.S. tax. To prevent abuse, tax credits are divided into *baskets* that separate passive income easily shifted to low-tax countries. Currently, two baskets exist, one for active income and one for passive income. More than half of foreign-source active business income is earned by firms with overall excess credits.[6]

Cross-crediting can also occur across types of income. For example, royalties are subject to current U.S. taxes and are generally deductible by firms in foreign jurisdictions, but they are considered foreign-source income. As a result, they are shielded from tax in many cases by excess credits.

To address tax avoidance by shifting passive income into low-tax jurisdictions, Subpart F restricts the applicability of deferral in some situations. Subpart F provides that U.S. stockholders (e.g., parent firms) of foreign corporations are subject to current U.S. tax on certain types of subsidiary income, whether or not the income is repatriated. Only stockholders owning at least 10% of subsidiary stock and only subsidiaries that are at least 50% owned by 10% U.S. stockholders are subject to Subpart F. Countries that have territorial tax systems generally also have some type of anti-abuse provision to protect their tax bases.

Tax deferral results in heightened importance for the system's rules for dividing income between related firms; the more income a firm can assign, for tax purposes, to a foreign subsidiary in a low-tax country, the lower its overall tax burden. The current system generally requires firms to set hypothetical *transfer prices*, which are required to approximate the prices two firms would agree on if they conducted their transactions at arm's length. The system is complex and difficult to administer.

The foreign tax credit's limitation also places pressure on the system's rules for determining the source of income (*sourcing* rules). Because firms can only credit foreign taxes against the portion of taxable income attributable to foreign sources, taxpayers must assign both revenue and costs to either domestic or foreign sources. Although the tax code contains rules for making such allocations, they are likewise complex and difficult to administer.

In sum, the United States taxes its resident corporations on their worldwide income but permits indefinite deferral of active business income earned through foreign subsidiaries. Where U.S. taxes apply, foreign tax credits alleviate double taxation but are limited to offsetting U.S. tax on foreign income. Subpart F is designed to deny deferral to what is generally passive income.

Possible Revisions

Because the current U.S. tax system is a mix of a worldwide system and a territorial system, the fundamental tax reform issue is whether moving toward either pure system—a territorial or worldwide residence-based regime—would be an improvement. Moving toward a territorial system would involve permanently exempting most foreign-source active business income. (Most territorial proposals, however, would continue taxing passive income, as under current law's Subpart F.) Moving toward a worldwide tax would eliminate the deferral benefit and might also entail further restricting cross-crediting by increasing the number of baskets for the foreign tax credit limit. Some revisions that maintain the current system but tighten the rules for deductions include proposals to disallow certain deductions of the parent company (such as interest) that reflect the share of income that is deferred.

The report defers discussion of the precise changes fundamental reform would entail. First, however, it explains the tools economists have developed for evaluating the various international tax systems.

Neutrality, Efficiency, and Competitiveness

The term *competitiveness* has often been invoked in the debate about U.S. policy in a global economy, including discussions of U.S. tax policy.[7] In economic analysis, however, it is not *countries* that are competitive; it is *companies* that are. A company generally thinks of itself as competitive if it can produce at the same cost as, or a lower cost than, other firms. But a country's firms cannot be competitive in all areas. Indeed, even if firms in a country are more productive than firms in all other countries in every respect, a country would still tend to produce those goods in which its relative advantage is greatest. The other countries need to produce goods with their resources as well. This notion is called comparative advantage, and it is an important concept in economic theory.[8]

When discussing national policy, including tax policy and its effect on the international allocation of capital, the issues are generally framed around questions of efficiency, neutrality, and optimal policies rather than notions of competitiveness. These terms can mean the same thing, or they can be slightly different. Neutrality generally refers to provisions that do not alter the allocation of investment from that which would occur without taxes. When markets are operating efficiently, a neutral tax policy will also be an efficient policy because it will maintain the efficient allocation that would occur without taxes. Moreover, even when the market is imperfect, neutrality may still be the policy most likely to be efficient, given the difficulty in identifying and measuring market imperfections.

Optimal policy differs from efficiency in that it usually refers to a particular agent or actor choosing a policy that maximizes his or her own welfare. A country can also choose a policy that leads to the greatest welfare for its own citizens, even if that policy distorts the allocation of capital (is not neutral) and leads to less efficient worldwide production. The optimal policy from the perspective of a country, in other words, may not be the most efficient in terms of the worldwide allocation of capital, and it may not be the optimal policy from the perspective of world economic welfare.

Economists have traditionally used three concepts to evaluate tax rules that apply to outbound investment. These concepts are referred to as neutrality concepts, although, as shown below, they are not always neutral in the sense of not distorting the allocation of investment. The concepts are capital export neutrality, capital import neutrality, and national neutrality. To evaluate the consequences of any multinational tax reform, it is crucial to understand these concepts, whether they are valid, and what they imply for policy. The concepts were developed when virtually all foreign investment took place as direct investment of multinational companies; virtually no foreign portfolio investment (ownership of foreign stock by U.S. citizens) existed. The growth in this portfolio investment has led to a new neutrality concept, referred to as capital ownership neutrality. These traditional and new concepts are addressed in turn.

Understanding Capital Export Neutrality, Capital Import Neutrality, and National Neutrality

Capital export neutrality requires a country to apply the same tax rate to its firms' investments, regardless of where they are located, and is embodied in a residence-based tax system. Capital import neutrality requires the same tax on firms with different nationalities that invest in a given location and is embodied in a territorial or source-based tax. National neutrality requires that the nation's total return on investment, including both that nation's taxes and its firms' profits, is equal in each jurisdiction, foreign and domestic. This form of neutrality is obtained by taxing foreign-source income and allowing a deduction for foreign taxes.

Some of these neutrality rules may also be rules for optimization. National neutrality is often described as optimal, but that outcome is only the case with perfectly mobile capital and no retaliation by foreign countries. There is also an optimizing rule for choosing the tax rate on inbound investment, which depends on how responsive that investment inflow is to the return.

Evaluating policy, discussed subsequently, is complicated because although some countries have territorial or source-based taxes, no country imposes a pure residence-based tax. Worldwide taxation as practiced in the United States and other countries has some attributes of a residence-based tax, but it is a mixture of residence- and source-based tax. Tax is imposed on foreign firms operating within the United States, a source-based attribute. On outbound investment, the application of tax to repatriated income creates some resemblance to residence tax, but the foreign tax credit limitations cause it to depart from such a tax, and deferral provisions introduce an element of a source-based tax.

Because these concepts are so frequently misunderstood, it is useful to employ a simple illustrative example to explain them with the pure tax systems that are consistent with capital export neutrality and capital import neutrality. In these simple systems, national neutrality is the same as capital export neutrality. Its nuances will be discussed in the following section, in which more realistic tax systems are discussed. In this instance, it may be helpful to demonstrate the difference between residence-based and source-based taxes in achieving economic neutrality.

Consider a world beginning with no taxes and assume that capital is perfectly substitutable across countries, implying that a firm will earn the same after-tax return in each location. The return is 10%. There are three countries: a high-tax country that imposes a 50% tax rate, a low-tax country that imposes a 25% tax rate, and a zero-tax country. All investment is made through the companies' direct operations, so there is no substitution of capital across firms and the capital owned by each country is fixed. The high- and low-tax countries have capital that can be used to invest in their own country or in the other two countries. To simplify, the zero-tax country is assumed to have only labor and no capital.

Table 1 shows the return to firms in the absence of any tax and with the two tax systems in place but before investment has shifted (which would alter the pretax return). Residence taxation, which produces capital export neutrality, has no effect on the allocation of investment by either country's firms because each firm still earns the same return in each location. Source-based taxation, however, will result in higher returns in the zero- and, to a lesser extent, low-tax countries. As a result, capital will flow out of the high-tax country, raising its return and lowering the wages of the workers in that country, and into the zero-tax country, lowering its return and raising the wages of the workers in that country. The effect on the low-tax country depends on the size of that country and its labor force relative to the rest of the world. In addition to the effects on the return to capital and wages, output is produced inefficiently, which reduces world welfare.

Table 1. Illustration of the Effects of Residence- and Source-Based Taxation

	Return by Location of Investment (%)		
Nationality of Firm	High-Tax Country	Low-Tax Country	Zero-Tax Country
No Taxes			
High-Tax Country	10%	10%	10%
Low-Tax Country	10%	10%	10%
Residence Tax			
High-Tax Country	5%	5%	5%
Low-Tax Country	7.5%	7.5%	7.5%
Source-Based (Territorial) Tax			
High-Tax Country	5%	7.5%	10%
Low-Tax Country	5%	7.5%	10%

Source: Compiled by the Congressional Research Service.

Note: The high-tax country has a 50% tax rate, whereas the low-tax country has a 25% tax rate.

Table 1 can also be used to show that the residence-based system is consistent with national neutrality but the source-based system is not. For the high-tax country, in each location it earns 5% in tax revenue and 5% in profits (for a total of 10%). Thus, the total return to the nation is equated in each jurisdiction. The same is true of the low-tax country, although the total return is split into 2.5% taxes and 7.5% profits. The source-based system does not meet that standard. Even before investment shifts, the high-tax country, while earning 10% domestically and in the zero-tax country, is earning only 7.5% in the low-tax country, because that country's government is collecting the tax. The same is true of the low-tax country with respect to investment taxed by the high-tax country.

National neutrality departs from capital export neutrality in the more complex, real-world circumstances. It, in fact, requires that foreign-source income be taxed and that any taxes imposed by the country of location be deducted (rather than the current rule of some countries, including the United States, that allow taxes to be credited). If foreign countries impose taxes, national neutrality does not lead to worldwide neutrality because foreign investment is discouraged in countries that impose taxes.

National neutrality is really about optimal policy, which maximizes the welfare of the country's residents. It is an optimal policy if all capital is perfectly mobile; if not, it is actually optimal for a country to impose even more tax on outbound investment than is suggested by the neutrality standard.

In sum, according to these long-standing measures of neutrality and efficiency, capital export neutrality is appropriate for maximizing world output, national neutrality is appropriate for maximizing a nation's welfare, and capital import "neutrality" is not neutral at all.

Capital Ownership Neutrality

A new concept of neutrality has appeared in recent years. The term capital ownership neutrality (CON) is closely associated with Desai and Hines, professors, respectively, of business at Harvard and economics at the University of Michigan.[9] The term itself, however, appears to have been coined by Michael Devereux,[10] a British economist. The underlying justification for the new standard's development, the growth of portfolio investment, was also discussed independently about the same time in a paper by Frisch.[11] Essentially, capital ownership neutrality is the same as capital import neutrality in that, under certain very restrictive assumptions, it is achieved by source-based taxation. Some of the earlier discussions viewed it as a resurrection of capital import neutrality.[12]

The issue of ownership neutrality developed because international investment markets changed. At the time the previous notions of neutral international tax systems were first developed— generally, the early 1960s— virtually all U.S. investment abroad was carried out through foreign direct investment by U.S. firms.[13] U.S. portfolio investors held almost no stock in foreign firms. Until the mid-1980s, the share of foreign stocks in U.S. residents' stock portfolios was less than 1%. Thus, it was reasonable to assume, as in the discussion above, that there was no substitution across the nationality of firms but rather only across locations—that is, U.S. investors could not substitute investment abroad through foreign firms for investment in U.S. firms with foreign operations. Over time, however, the share of foreign stock in U.S. residents' portfolios increased. By the end of 2006, before the recession, it was 22%. By the end of 2013, it was 18%, although that fall may have reflected the rest of the world's slower recovery from the recession.[14] This overall increase did not occur smoothly: it rose in the latter part of the mid-1980s to about 6%, leveled out for a number of years, then again increased around 1993 and 1994 to about 11%, where it stayed until around 2001 and then rose again.

A closer look at the CON concept indicates that, to make the argument that capital ownership neutrality (and therefore source-based taxation) should be the guiding principle for an efficient and neutral tax system, three requirements are needed. First, firms are assumed not to substitute operations in one location for those in another—capital is completely immobile across locations. Second, firms must differ in their productivity—that is, some firms are more efficient than others—and there must be substitution across portfolios that results in firms being shut out of lines of business that they could run more efficiently. Third, there must be no mechanisms available to obtain the benefits of productive efficiency—short of owning the productive capital assets. For example, relatively inefficient firms cannot rent efficient technologies or hire efficient managers away from efficient firms.

If only the first requirement is met (immobility across locations), any system of taxing investment abroad would be neutral because the particular distortion—allocation of investment across locations—is simply assumed away. It does not matter if overseas operations are taxed higher or lower than domestic investment, because investment has no reason to move. Residence taxation would be efficient as well as source-based taxation, because the national affiliation of firms would not matter to productivity (although residence taxation would not be optimal for the high-tax country that would have no revenues).[15]

If the two remaining assumptions also apply—productivity differs and no mechanisms exist to boost efficiency—it can be shown that residence-based taxation is inefficient whereas source-based taxation produces efficiency. For example, returning to *Table 1*, suppose some firms in each country are particularly productive and can earn 12% before tax rather than 10%. With residence-based taxation, the after-tax return of the high-tax country's productive firms, which would yield an after-tax return of 6%, would not be enough for these firms to operate and, if the only way to realize the higher return is to own the capital, the higher pretax yields of these more efficient firms would not be realized. With source-based taxation, the efficient firms in each country would operate and displace the less efficient ones.

In the more realistic tax systems in which countries also tax capital income in their own locations, the high-tax country's especially productive firms would still operate in their own country. That is, by taxing income within its borders, a high-tax country that is attempting to practice capital export neutrality with a worldwide tax still faces neutral ground in its home country. Thus, any distortion arising in practice from the current system would involve foreign firms and the solution of exempting foreign-source income from tax is the solution consistent with capital ownership neutrality.

Consider each of the restrictions in turn. The first is the assumption that capital is immobile across locations; as noted above, there is considerable evidence that it is not and, indeed, that it is quite elastic. So at best, it would be a question of picking which type of distortion is worse. As long as capital is mobile across jurisdictions, capital ownership neutrality is not neutral. At most, the model shows that there is no way to achieve neutrality and that one is in a second-best world.

The second restriction requires a high, perhaps perfect, degree of substitution in portfolios of different types of stocks that would lead to the exclusion of stock of high-tax countries. There is considerable evidence to suggest that such perfect substitution is not the case. It has long been known that there is a significant home bias in the holding of both portfolio and direct assets. Despite global securities markets, American residents continue to hold 80% of their stock portfolios in stock of U.S. firms. If portfolio investment were perfectly substitutable, the U.S. share would be expected to be closer to the share of total assets. The U.S. accounts for about a third of total fixed investment of the Organization for Economic Cooperation and Development (OECD) countries.[16]

The fact that the share of foreign stocks in the portfolios of U.S. residents has grown does not in itself provide evidence of a significant elasticity; rather, it may reflect a variety of technical and institutional changes that make holding foreign stocks more feasible or more likely. Moreover, the portfolio shares are consistent with the notion that the holdings that do exist are not due so much to tax differences as to a general desire to diversify assets across countries to reduce cyclical risk. Prior to the recession, two-thirds of investment in foreign equities by U.S. residents was in other countries with similar tax rates. At the end of 2006, the two largest shares of total foreign equities in U.S. residents' portfolios were for the United Kingdom (16%) and Japan (15%). The UK, with a 30% corporate rate, had a lower statutory rate than the United States (39% including state taxes), but Japan had a rate of 41%. Although both rates subsequently fell relative to U.S. rates, the UK share remained about the same at the end of 2013, whereas the share for Japan fell to 9%. The next two largest claimants in 2006 (Canada and France, with 7% and 6%, respectively) had tax rates of 35% each. These shares were similar at the end of 2013 (6% and 5%). Canada's tax rate had declined, but France's was unchanged.[17] There were significant shares in two tax havens in 2006, Bermuda (5%) and the Cayman Islands (3%). According to the 2006 Department of Treasury report, however, the Bermuda investments are largely former U.S. firms that have moved their locations to avoid U.S. tax (a phenomenon called inversion that was subsequently addressed with legislative restrictions) and the Cayman Islands investments are in offshore financial centers (again, likely a tax-avoidance issue rather than a direct-production issue).[18] The share in Bermuda declined to 3% at the end of 2013, but the Cayman Islands share rose to 10%, apparently because of the addition of new survey respondents. The Cayman Islands was also an inversion location.

An imperfect portfolio substitution elasticity also suggests that the phenomenon of eliminating efficient firms is less likely to happen. Especially productive and efficient firms will earn higher returns than other firms in similar circumstances of nationality and location, and they would be expected to be retained in both domestic and foreign investors' portfolios. Any firms whose size is contracted by portfolio shifts due to tax rates are more likely to be the marginal firms that have a normal level of productivity.

Finally, this model assumes there are no other ways to enjoy the additional productivity of more efficient firms. In effect, the model begins with the assumption of productive advantages without defining in formal terms—so that the effects can be modeled—the source of the productivity.

For example, if the greater productivity of the firm is due to the employment of managers with greater skills, then that productivity arises at a cost, and these management skills embodied in the individuals resident in a given country should be free to move to their highest use and allocated efficiently. Because they add a surplus value, they would not be driven out of the market, and worldwide efficiency requires a capital export neutrality approach to labor resources as well as capital.

If the asset is uniquely tied to the firm—such as a value through a trademark, intangible research and development, or even a management set-up—the model does not allow for the fact that ownership of the productive assets and ownership of the intangible asset can, in most cases, be separated.

Trademarks and patents can be franchised and sold. Or, if the intangible cannot be separately sold (for example, if the research and development could be easily copied and thus is not patented but kept secret), there are ways for the firm to operate without ownership of the capital assets, such as factories, machinery, and equipment that give rise to normal products. These assets could be leased by the firm with the intangible asset. Moreover, if the asset is not closely tied to management, the firm could arrange for contract manufacturing, a technique commonly used to shift profits. These techniques may be less than perfect if there are principal-agent costs,[19] but this effect is of questionable importance.

In light of the many ways in which the efficiency costs of capital ownership non-neutrality are unlikely to be significant compared to location distortions, it seems questionable to use meeting this standard of neutrality to evaluate tax reform changes and questionable to see source-based taxation as an efficient international tax regime.

ASSESSING THE EXISTING TAX SYSTEM

The above examples illustrate the various traditional concepts of neutrality and how they are embodied in basic tax structures. However, as described at the report's outset, the U.S. tax system is a hybrid—neither a pure territorial- or residence-based system. Accordingly, it presents a patchwork of incentive effects, sometimes posing an incentive to invest abroad and, in other situations, presenting either a disincentive or tax neutrality. This section looks at the existing system's principal incentive effects.

First, in some cases the U.S. system resembles residence-based taxation—it taxes foreign branch income on a current basis while allowing a foreign tax credit. Even where current taxation applies, however, the U.S. system departs from pure residence taxation by placing a limit on its foreign tax credit. If pure residence-based taxation means taxing income of residents at the same rate, regardless of where it is earned, an unlimited foreign tax credit would be required. Under such a credit, when the foreign tax is lower than the home country tax, the home country would collect a residual, equating the total tax imposed to that on its domestic investment. When the foreign country's tax is higher, the home country would have to refund the excess so that, again, the tax on the foreign investment would be the same as the tax on domestic investment. In practice, however, an unlimited foreign tax credit is not feasible because of its potential threat to the home country tax base (here, that of the

United States). Without a limit, countries host to foreign investment could simply raise their taxes on inbound investment without limit and without fear of driving foreign investors away. The foreign investors could simply credit their high foreign taxes against their home country tax bill. The United States thus limits its foreign tax credit to offsetting U.S. taxes on foreign (and not domestic) income.

The incentive effects of a worldwide system with a limited credit depend on exactly how the credit is limited. If the limit applies separately for each country (a *per-country* limit), the system would achieve neutrality on outbound investment with respect to low tax-rate countries but not high tax-rate countries. If taxes can be averaged across countries—that is, if a firm calculates a single limit aggregated across countries—the neutrality consequences are less clear. In that case, the excess credits from the investment in a high-tax country can be used to offset tax due on investments in the low-tax country (can be cross-credited). For example, assume profits were $100 in a high-tax location with a 50% rate and $100 in the zero-tax location, with the home country tax rate 25%. With no cross-crediting, a firm from the 25% tax rate country uses the foreign tax of $50 to wipe out the home country tax of $25, with only the tax of $50 applying, while the firm would pay a home country tax of $25 on the income earned in the zero-tax jurisdiction. The total tax is $75. With cross-crediting, the total foreign-source income is $200, the total foreign tax paid is $50 (in the high-tax country, on $100 of profit), and the total home-country tax due is also $50 (25% of $200 of income in both countries). All foreign tax is credited and the total tax is $50.

Cross-crediting, as allowed in the U.S. tax system, can therefore reduce the disincentive to invest in high-tax countries if the firm already has investment in the zero-tax country because the excess credits have a value. Similarly, it can increase the incentive to invest in the zero-tax country if the firm already has investment in the high-tax country because excess credits can effectively remove any residual tax in the zero-tax country. In either case, foreign investment is encouraged relative to domestic investment. In practice, the U.S. tax system permits extensive cross-crediting; it does not require a per-country limitation, although it does require firms to calculate separate limits for passive and active business income.

Second, the U.S. tax system departs from residence-based taxation in its use of deferral. As described above, U.S. taxes generally do not apply to the foreign business income of foreign-chartered subsidiaries. This feature of the tax system introduces elements of a territorial or source-based taxation into the system, and it also introduces a distortion in firms' decisions of whether to return profits to the United States or reinvest them abroad. Moreover, the interaction of deferral with cross-crediting provides some scope for firms to choose the times and places of repatriation to minimize tax liability. In general, the availability of deferral—like the territorial taxation it at least approaches—poses an incentive for U.S. firms to invest in low-tax countries. In addition, once capital has been invested abroad, the provision encourages firms to retain their earnings overseas rather than returning them to the United States.[20]

This mixture of treatments also provides methods for avoiding tax apart from the direct effects on investment allocation. Deferral provides an incentive to artificially shift profits to low-tax jurisdictions. Because firms can choose between branch operations and investment via foreign-chartered subsidiaries, they can use a branch form when operations are starting up and typically lose money to allow losses to be deducted from the U.S. worldwide income tax and then shift to a subsidiary form when the operation becomes profitable.

In sum, the current system poses a patchwork of incentive effects that is in keeping with its hybrid nature. Where current taxation applies—for example, to branch income—there is a disincentive to invest in high-tax countries and either an incentive or neutrality toward investment in low-tax countries, depending on whether the investing firm can use cross-crediting of foreign taxes. Where deferral is available, the system poses an incentive to invest in low-tax countries. It also provides mechanisms for artificially sheltering income from tax.

TERRITORIAL TAXATION: THE DIVIDEND EXEMPTION PROPOSAL

The preceding sections showed why the theoretical argument that territorial taxation is optimal is difficult to defend.[21] Some have argued, however, that although territorial taxation may not be the most efficient system in a perfect world, it is nonetheless superior to the hybrid, patchwork system that is the current U.S. system—a *second-best* argument.

To understand this argument for territorial taxation, it is helpful to examine the specific version proposed in a 2001 American Enterprise Institute monograph by economists Harry Grubert and John Mutti. Until the recent proposals for a territorial tax by Ways and Means Committee Chairman Camp and Senator Enzi, the proposal that was discussed over the years was the Grubert-Mutti proposal. In 2005, President Bush's advisory commission on tax reform set forth a similar plan.[22] More recently, the National Commission on Fiscal Responsibility and Reform proposed a territorial tax, although it did not provide specific details.[23] It is useful to discuss the Grubert-Mutti plan first and then address how the two more recent proposals differed from it.[24]

Grubert and Mutti described their proposal as a "dividend exemption" system, thus focusing on the chief modification their plan would make to the current regime: it would exempt from U.S. taxes dividends repatriated to U.S. parents from foreign subsidiary corporations, thus moving from current law's deferral for foreign income to a permanent exemption. More generally, an exemption system can be viewed as a territorial tax system whose application is restricted to active business investment abroad but that continues to tax portfolio investment of firms (such as interest, royalties, and similar income) on a current basis.

Several additional features of the plan are important to the advantages it might have over the current system. First, the plan would not permit foreign tax credits to be claimed for foreign taxes paid with respect to repatriated earnings. The repatriations, after all, would be exempt from U.S. tax, thus obviating the need for relief from double taxation. Second, deductions allocable to tax-exempt foreign-source income would be disallowed. Here, the reasoning is that the purpose of deductions is to remove items of cost from the tax base; because overseas income would no longer be in the U.S. tax base, removal of associated costs would not be necessary. Importantly, this would mean that a portion of debt incurred by a U.S. parent corporation would not be deductible—the portion assumed to be used in financing tax-exempt foreign subsidiaries. This limitation on deductions would also apply to other overhead expenses, including research and development costs.

As described in the preceding sections, the capital import neutrality and capital ownership neutrality standards both recommend adoption of territorial taxation, but traditional economic theory is skeptical of the theoretical justification of the two standards. Grubert and Mutti argue, however, that even if capital import neutrality and capital ownership neutrality are rejected on theoretical grounds, an exemption system is superior to the current hybrid system in terms of several important factors: efficiency, simplicity, and the raising of tax revenue.

First, efficiency: Grubert and Mutti argue that current law's application of tax to repatriated foreign earnings encourages wasteful and inefficient behavior on the part of corporations in devising methods of repatriating foreign earnings without paying U.S. tax. Under an exemption system, such wasteful planning would be unnecessary. In addition, because foreign tax credits would no longer be applicable, cross-crediting of excess foreign tax credits would no longer shield investment in low-tax foreign locations from U.S. tax and the artificial diversion of technology-exploiting investment to low-tax locations would no longer occur.[25] The elimination of credits would also increase the tax on royalties, which are subject to current tax but considered foreign-source income and thus can have their U.S. tax liability offset by excess credits.

Nevertheless, elimination of these sources of inefficiency alone would not be sufficient to make an exemption system less wasteful than current law. If elimination of tax on repatriations were the only feature of an exemption system, the system would likely increase inefficiency by encouraging added investment in low-tax countries. Rather, the crucial element to an exemption system's purported superiority is its elimination of interest and other overhead deductions for overseas investment. The inclusion of this provision would actually result in an increase in the average tax burden for overseas investment, thus generating an efficiency gain from an improved allocation of investment away from low-tax overseas locations and into the domestic economy.[26]

An exemption system may also increase tax revenue. The Grubert and Mutti analysis concludes that the system would generate $7.7 billion annually in added U.S. revenue.[27] (Their estimate is based on 1994 data.) More recently, the Joint Committee on Taxation (JCT) estimated the revenue gain at about $7 billion per year.[28] As with the efficiency gains, however, the increase in tax revenues is crucially dependent on denial of deductions for costs allocated to tax-exempt foreign income. Without the new restrictions, an exemption system would likely reduce tax revenue. Moreover, the JCT has significantly increased estimates of the cost of deferral, from approximately $6 billion in 2006 to more than $80 billion in FY2014, making it more likely that the Grubert-Mutti proposal would lose revenue.[29] A loss of revenue would generally indicate that foreign investment is favored in the aggregate.

In the area of simplicity, proponents of an exemption system emphasize its reduction in the need for tax planning. Note, however, that tax complexity—and its accompanying difficulties for tax administration—exists when entities or activities are taxed according to different rules. Under an exemption system, foreign subsidiary corporations would be tax exempt as under current law, and because the exemption would be permanent rather than temporary, its import for firms' tax planners would be magnified. Accordingly, the tax system's transfer pricing rules for allocating income among U.S. parent firms and their foreign subsidiaries would become more important; more pressure would apply to rules that are inherently difficult to enforce. The same would be true for the distinction between active and passive income, because active income would be permanently exempt and passive-investment income would be taxed on a current basis. Firms would have an even greater incentive to move from branch to subsidiary operations for start-up firms.

In an article critical of territorial tax proposals, Kleinbard pointed out analyses by Grubert and others that emphasized the growth in the importance of royalties as a share of repatriated earnings for multinationals, suggesting that the exploitation of intangible assets by multinationals in foreign locations is increasing. However, whereas the Grubert and Mutti analysis sees this as an important reason to adopt an exemption system—cross-crediting of foreign taxes would no longer pose an incentive to low-tax investment under an exemption system—Kleinbard sees it as a liability. The growth of intangibles, argues Kleinbard, would place enormous pressure on the administration of transfer prices.[30]

Proponents of an exemption system concede that it is not perfect but argue that it is at least superior to the highly imperfect existing system. Even this defense, however, has its shortcomings: the most economically attractive aspects of the exemption proposal could, in principle, be adopted piecemeal, and its most distortionary aspects could be left behind. Specifically, more restrictive rules for deducting interest and other costs could be adopted without exempting dividend repatriations from U.S. tax. Such plans could enhance economic efficiency more than would the full-blown exemption systems.

More recent proposals, such as a discussion draft by the Ways and Means Committee subsequently included in a proposal by Ways and Means Chairman Camp, subsequently introduced as H.R. 1 in the 113th Congress,[31] and a bill by Senator Enzi (S. 2091, 112th Congress), were similar in many ways but also differ substantially from the Grubert-Mutti proposal.

Chairman Camp's proposal had an allocation of interest rather than all deductions, and S. 2091 had no allocation of deductions. Both bills provided some relief for royalties. These proposals also contained anti-base erosion provisions or options for limiting profit shifting whose effectiveness is uncertain. They excluded only 95% of dividends, a provision intended to capture some overhead costs but one that is much smaller than the full overhead costs.[32]

The Camp proposal and S. 2091 included provisions aimed at limiting profit shifting through transfers of intangibles by providing a minimum tax on foreign intangible income (which also applied to royalties). In addition, they included an allocation of interest deductions. The proposed plans were revenue neutral in the budget horizon, but this neutrality relied on a one-time taxation of existing accumulated earnings and thus would have lost revenue in the long run.[33] This loss of revenue suggests that both the Camp and Enzi proposals would likely have encouraged more investment abroad. The fleshing out of a detailed territorial tax provision that might be considered legislatively has also served to highlight one of the major concerns about moving to a territorial tax: the possible increase in international profit shifting and tax avoidance, discussed below.[34]

As noted above, the Camp proposal also included a tax on prior accumulated deferred income with a 90% exclusion for earnings not held in cash and a 75% exclusion for earnings held in cash. The proposal also reduced the corporate tax rate to 25%, making these rates 2.5% and 6.25%. Proportional foreign tax credits would have been allowed.

The report next examines what moving toward a residence-based system would look like in practice.

A Residence-Based System in Practice

The capital export neutrality standard recommends a system that would be based on residence— that is, a system that taxes the income of home-country firms, regardless of where it is earned. This section looks at the shape a residence-based system would likely take.

Current law's deferral system would be repealed under a residence-based system, and U.S. taxation would apply on a current basis to the income of foreign subsidiaries, whether or not the income is repatriated. If it were not for foreign taxes, deferral's repeal would move the system to the brink of capital export neutrality (except for the portfolio investment concern): the tax burden on foreign investment would roughly equal the tax rate on domestic investment. Foreign taxes, however, complicate matters and make pure capital export neutrality difficult to achieve in practice. The problem arises when a foreign host country's tax rate exceeds the U.S. domestic tax rate. In such cases, pure capital export neutrality would require an unlimited foreign tax credit. Foreign taxes would offset U.S. taxes on domestic as well as foreign income—only by this mechanism could the high foreign tax burden be brought into line with taxes on domestic investment. Yet, as noted in the preceding section on the existing tax system, an unlimited foreign tax credit is impractical because foreign governments could, in effect, draw on the U.S. Treasury by raising taxes on U.S. investors ad infinitum.

Advocates of a residence-based system have in some cases called for a more restrictive form of the foreign tax credit limitation that would place more limits on cross-crediting than does current law's two-part limit. For example, at various times in the past, the United States has required firms to calculate their limitation on a country-by-country basis (a per-country limitation) under which taxes paid to one country could not be credited against U.S. tax on income from another country.[35] The Wyden-Gregg Tax Reform Act, S. 3018, introduced in the 111th Congress, would have, in the context of a general corporate reform that broadened the base and reduced the rate, eliminated deferral, and instituted a per-country foreign tax credit limit. A similar bill, S. 727, was sponsored by Wyden and Coats and introduced in the 112th Congress. An alternative or additional approach to restricting cross-crediting was implemented by the Tax Reform Act of 1986 (P.L. 99- 514), which, instead of requiring separate limits for each country, specified a variety of different types of income for which separate limits (baskets) were required. The American Jobs Creation Act of 2004 (AJCA; P.L. 108-357), however, reduced the number of separate limits to current law's two.[36] Note, however, that a more restrictive foreign tax credit limitation would not necessarily move a residence-based system closer to pure capital export neutrality. As noted above, cross-crediting may pose an incentive to invest in low-tax countries, but it also mitigates the disincentive to invest in high-tax countries.

Capital export neutrality requires equal tax burdens on foreign and domestic investment. Several features of the current system favor domestic over foreign investment, and modifying these features would move the current system in the direction of capital export neutrality. The most important of these is the 9% tax deduction for domestic production enacted in 2004 by AJCA. Other tax benefits that are restricted to domestic investment include the Section 179 "expensing" allowance for machines and equipment and the research and experimentation tax credit.

As noted above, Grubert and Altshuler revisited the topic of international tax reform in 2006. In their analysis, they compared the exemption system with what they termed a "burden neutral" worldwide taxation system. In constructing this latter system, they couple elimination of deferral with a reduction in the statutory U.S. tax rate that applies to foreign earnings—thus using the added tax revenue from deferral's repeal to, in effect, *purchase* a cut in the tax rate. The goal of the exchange is to not damage what they term the "competitive position" of U.S. multinationals. As a consequence of the countervailing changes, the burden on investment in a range of low-tax countries would increase; the burden of a range of income that is repatriated under current law would fall, but the overall burden on overseas investment would be unchanged.

Grubert and Altshuler note that the overall advantage of their burden-neutral worldwide proposal over current law depends on outcomes that are, as yet, unknown: how many firms would be in an excess-credit position under the plan and what the burden-neutral tax rate would be. They also caution that the plan would have another weakness—foreign countries would have an incentive to raise their tax rates in the face of current U.S. taxation because inbound U.S. investment would be less sensitive to the foreign rates.[37] They further note that their plan's reduction of tax rates at the corporate level would shift more of the overall U.S. tax burden on corporations from the corporate to the shareholder level—a virtue in the modern world in which capital is increasingly mobile because shareholder-level taxes are generally imposed on a residence basis and thus achieve allocative efficiency.

A Minimum Tax Approach

In 2013, then-Chairman Baucus of the Senate Finance Committee released a discussion draft of a proposal that taxed some foreign-source income in full and provided lower rates on others, while retaining the foreign tax credit.[38] Under the plan, income derived from activities with a U.S. source as well as passive and mobile income (presumably similar to current Subpart F income) would be taxed in full when earned. Other foreign-source income would also be taxed when earned but at a rate lower than the U.S. rate. The discussion draft described two options, one in which this income would be taxed at 80% of the U.S. rate and one in which active income would be taxed at 60% of the U.S. rate and other income at 100%. The 80% and 60% figures were only suggestions. Minimum tax approaches had also been suggested, without specifics, by the President.[39]

A minimum tax on foreign-source income might be a compromise between moving to a territorial system and eliminating deferral or imposing stricter rules in the context of the current system. Another form of compromise might be requiring a percentage of income to be paid out. This type of system would eliminate the repatriation tax because income would be taxed (at some rate) regardless of repatriation.

The discussion draft also included provisions aimed at limiting profit shifting, including an interest-allocation rule (similar to that of Grubert and Mutti) that would disallow deductions associated with exempt income.

The Baucus staff proposal also included a 20% tax on prior deferred earnings with a proportional foreign tax credit allowed.

The President's budget proposal for FY2016 included a minimum tax of 19% on income of controlled foreign corporations in each country, along with a number of other revisions that had been in prior budgets.[40] A foreign tax credit equal to 85% of taxes paid with taxes assigned per country based on tax residence (not incorporation) would be allowed. The proposal also allows an exemption from the minimum tax base for an allowance for corporate equity (ACE). This provision allows a risk-free return on active assets invested in the country. Its purpose is to exempt from the minimum tax return on the actual activities in the country. The proposal included some other anti-abuse provisions (see below).

The proposal also included a 14% tax on prior deferred earnings, with a proportional foreign tax credit.

PROPOSALS TO RESTRICT DEFERRAL AND CROSS-CREDITING

It is also possible to move toward further restrictions on deferral without eliminating it entirely. One such proposal, contained in H.R. 3970, a tax-reform plan introduced in 2007 by Chairman Rangel of the Ways and Means Committee, would disallow certain deductions of parent-company costs (the most important being interest) that reflect the share of income that is deferred. This provision, projected to raise revenue of $106 billion over 10 years, would make investment in low-tax countries much less attractive.[41] The revenue from this provision and other changes were to be used to lower the corporate statutory tax rate.

This proposal also included a foreign tax credit pooling proposal, which would allow a share of foreign tax credits equal to the share of income repatriated. This provision limits the ability of firms to repatriate income from high-tax countries and use excess foreign tax credits to shield income from low-tax countries from the foreign tax credit.

President Obama has proposed these two changes, along with others, in his various budget outlines from 2009 through 2014.[42] (The allocation of deductions, however, excluded research and development expenditures and focused on interest deductions). In the FY2015 budget, the deferral provision was projected to raise $5.0 billion in FY2016 and $43.8 billion over 10 years

(FY2015-FY2024), and the foreign credit pooling provision was projected to raise $6.7 billion in FY2016 and $74.6 billion over 10 years. These provisions were not included in his FY20016 budget because that proposal included the minimum tax proposed above.

Another provision (contained in the FY2010 proposals but not in later outlines) would eliminate *check-the-box*, a provision that allows firms to elect to treat subsidiaries as separate entities or disregarded entities and permits firms to avoid current taxation on certain income that would be subject to Subpart F anti-abuse rules (such as interest on loans from a subsidiary in a low-tax country to a related subsidiary in a high-tax country). This provision was originally projected to raise $86 billion over 10 years.[43]

A provision in the FY2015 budget proposal would treat excess income from intangibles as Subpart F income and assign them to a separate foreign tax credit basket. This provision was projected to raise $2.67 billion in FY2016 and $30.0 billion over 10 years.

A number of additional proposals that raised revenues on foreign-source income were included in the earlier budget outlines and continued in the later ones, including provisions to restrict credits for payments that are considered in the nature of royalties on extractive industries and to limit deductions for reinsurance of insurance companies via foreign subsidiaries. The FY2015 budget outline included some new provisions to tax under Subpart F certain income associated with digital goods and certain sales income.

The FY2015 proposal also included a new provision to address the allocation of interest to U.S. subsidiaries of foreign parents (replacing one to apply this interest restriction to inverted firms that had shifted headquarters abroad),[44] an issue addressing inbound rather than outbound investment. This provision was also in the FY2016 budget. This provision was projected to raise $2.6 billion in FY2016 and $64.2 billion over 10 years. In addition, the FY2015 and FY2016 proposals contained a provision to disallow inversions (shifting from U.S. to foreign headquarters) by merging with a smaller company, projected to raise $0.3 billion in FY2016 and $12.8 billion over 10 years.[45]

The earlier proposals included a provision that would disallow foreign tax credits when the associated income is not received, as can occur with an arrangement termed a *reverse hybrid*. This provision was adopted in 2010 (P.L. 111-226). P.L. 111-226 contained a number of provisions directed at perceived abuses of the foreign tax credit.[46]

The Administration earlier presented a framework for tax reform that mentioned five elements: the allocation of interest for deferred income, a tax on excess intangibles, a minimum tax on foreign-source income in low-tax countries, disallowing a deduction for the cost of moving abroad, and providing a 20% credit for costs of moving an operation from abroad to the United States.[47] All of these provisions were included in the FY2016 budget proposal.

A minimum tax on foreign-source income, as discussed above, might be a compromise between moving to a territorial system and eliminating deferral. Another form of compromise might be requiring a percentage of income to be paid out.

TAX HAVENS: ISSUES AND POLICY OPTIONS

The topic of *tax havens* has been a focus of recent international tax policy discussions. (This topic is treated in more detail in another CRS report.)[48] Tax havens do not fit neatly into the traditional capital export neutrality/capital import neutrality/national neutrality evaluation framework outlined above—perhaps because the tax-haven issue involves as much artificial shifting of income and investment as it does questions about how investment is actually allocated. To the extent tax havens abet the shifting of income from its true geographic source to low-tax jurisdictions (the havens themselves), they raise questions about protecting the U.S. Treasury from revenue losses. They also raise questions about tax fairness (not all taxpayers are in position to reduce their U.S. taxes by using tax havens). And to the extent tax havens reduce the tax burden on investment that truly occurs overseas, they also raise the same questions about economic efficiency and neutrality addressed by the traditional framework outlined above.

Tax haven is not a precisely defined term, but in most usages it refers to a country—in many cases a small one—in which nonresidents can save taxes by conducting various investments, transactions, and activities. Attributes that make a country a successful tax haven include low or nonexistent tax rates applicable to foreigners; strict bank and financial secrecy laws; and a highly developed communications, financial, and legal infrastructure.

At the heart of the tax-haven issue is the discrepancy between real economic activity and what is only apparent. Much of the economic activity that appears to occur in tax havens actually occurs elsewhere and is only associated with particular tax-haven countries because of sometimes spurious relationships between the person or firm conducting the activity and the tax-haven country. Thus, for example, much (or even most) of the income reported by U.S.-controlled subsidiaries chartered in tax havens may well have its true economic location either in some other foreign country or in the United States itself. In several small tax-haven locations, incomes of U.S.-controlled foreign subsidiaries are many times larger than GDP.[49]

In part, U.S. firms may find tax havens useful tax-saving mechanisms because of particular aspects of the U.S. tax structure. Here, no illegal tax evasion or even transfer-price manipulation may be necessary to obtain tax savings. An example is the technique sometimes termed a corporate inversion reorganization, in which the overall parent of a corporate group shifts from a U.S.-chartered entity to a foreign corporation organized in an offshore tax haven. The rearrangement can potentially reduce or eliminate U.S. tax that would otherwise be due when foreign income is repatriated. Although legislation has been enacted to prevent inversions that involve simply moving the firm's headquarters, a number of firms recently announced plans to accomplish a headquarters shift by merging with a foreign firm of sufficient size (while still retaining control of the company) to avoid the U.S. law's restrictions. The President's budget proposal includes a provision addressing this issue, and legislative proposals have also been introduced.[50]

U.S. firms can also use tax havens to shift income out of foreign countries where there are corporate income taxes to the zero-tax environment many tax havens offer. Short of outright tax evasion, techniques for shifting income include manipulation of transfer prices affixed to intrafirm sales and other transfers, and the structuring of intra-firm lending and interest charges so as to shift income out of high-tax countries to tax havens (sometimes called *earnings stripping*). Transfer price manipulation can also theoretically be used to shift what is actually U.S.-source income to offshore-tax-haven subsidiary corporations. Some of the President's proposals and the Camp tax reform proposal address these issues.

Along with income shifting and expatriation by corporations, tax havens in some cases apparently abet the outright evasion of taxes, occasionally by U.S. citizens. For example, income from illegal activity in the United States can be shielded from U.S. authorities if a tax haven offers sufficient bank secrecy. Or, taxes on legally generated U.S. income are apparently evaded in some cases by depositing the income in secrecy-protected foreign bank accounts.[51] The focus of this report, however, is the activities of multinational firms, so its concern with tax havens is more with legal (albeit what some might term *abusive*) income shifting rather than with outright tax evasion.

In part, the ability of firms to divert income from other foreign locations to tax havens has implications for the real location of investment: just because a tax haven is not the true source of income does not make the associated tax savings any less real for the underlying investment, wherever it may be located. Interpret the effect of tax havens on actual investment in terms of the efficiency framework outlined in previous sections of the report. First, regarding the allocation of investment between the United States and foreign locations, existing data indicate that the United States is a relatively high-tax country, even if tax havens are omitted from the calculation.[52] Thus, much of the income shifted to tax havens is likely shifted from countries whose taxes are lower than U.S. taxes to begin with. As a result, it is likely that tax havens on balance magnify the distorting effects of deferral, thus further diverting U.S. investment to foreign locations and, in turn, reducing economic efficiency and U.S. national welfare. This efficiency effect, however, may be mitigated by a reduction in the tax-induced distortion of location decisions across foreign countries.[53]

Along with efficiency effects, tax havens reduce tax revenue collections by capital-exporting countries. In the case of U.S. firms' use of tax havens, the revenue loss can accrue both to the United States (in the case of income shifted from domestic sources) and other countries (in the case of income shifted from other countries with higher taxes). Tax havens likewise have the potential to damage perceptions of tax fairness when public reports appear of large firms and wealthy individuals using tax havens to avoid or evade substantial taxes.[54] Accordingly, a policy question is how tax evasion, or what might be termed *abusive* tax avoidance through tax havens, can be reduced.

One possible approach to tax havens is multilateral (that is, multicountry) action. The concept here is that tax havens flourish in part because of a lack of coordination in tax administration between non-haven countries and that efforts to suppress tax-haven activities cannot be successful without solidarity among non-haven countries.[55] One prominent multilateral effort has been the OECD's Project on Harmful Tax Practices, initiated in 1996. The focus of the OECD's project has been to identify tax havens and induce them to increase their "transparency" (presumably reduce secrecy about financial transactions) as well as to increase the number and scope of exchange of tax information agreements with tax havens.[56] The OECD more recently has been pursuing a broad effort to address profit shifting referred to as Base Erosion and Profit Shifting, or BEPs. A number of proposals have been issued.[57]

The Clinton Administration put forth a unilateral approach with its FY2001 budget proposal. The basis of the plan was to be a list of jurisdictions identified by the Treasury Department as tax havens. Foreign tax credits and the deferral benefit would be restricted for taxpayers using the identified tax havens.[58] More narrow unilateral approaches proposed in the past have primarily involved increasing information reporting requirements.

Several legislative proposals, including proposals in President Obama's budget and a number of congressional proposals, have been made to address evasion and avoidance. Some provisions were adopted in the Hire Act in 2010 (P.L. 111-147).[59]

General Reforms of the Corporate Tax and Implications for International Tax Treatment

Despite increasing globalization of the U.S. economy, foreign direct investment remains a small share of the U.S.-owned capital stock. For that reason, it would perhaps not be appropriate for international concerns to dominate the formulation of corporate tax policy. Nevertheless, specific forms of corporate tax revisions might have important consequences for international taxation.

Under the current U.S. system, taxes on corporate profits at the individual level (dividends and capital gains) tend to be collected (due to tax treaties) on a residence basis. If taxes at the individual level could be increased and taxes at the corporate level decreased, the tax would shift toward a residence-based system without any other changes and without any additional concerns about portfolio substitution. In 2003, relief for double taxation was provided by reducing the tax rate on corporate dividends from the ordinary tax rate to 15% for those in brackets above the 15% rate and to 5% for others. The 5% rate was then scheduled to fall to 0%. Capital gains, which formerly had a top rate of 20%, were also subjected to these lower rates. These provisions expired at the end of 2012 and were extended by the Tax Relief, Unemployment Insurance Reauthorization, and Job Creation Act of 2010 (P.L. 111-312). With the expiration of all the 2001 and 2003 tax cuts scheduled for the end of 2012, these lower rates were made permanent by the American Taxpayer Relief Act (P.L. 112-240), except that very high-income individuals ($450,000 of taxable income for joint returns and $400,000 for single returns), with whom much of capital gains is concentrated, were taxed at 20% on dividends and capital gains.

The revenue estimates for keeping lower rates compared with the return to pre-2003 treatment were $22 billion for dividends in FY2016 and $6.5 billion for capital gains.[60] Based on projected corporate revenues of $439 billion for that year,[61] returning to pre-2003 law would provide sufficient revenue to permit a 2.2 percentage point reduction in the corporate tax rate. The capital gains portion is small because it affected only a small part of capital gains, although it is slightly larger (by about $1 billion) than a static estimate because of scoring conventions that increase realizations substantially with tax reductions.[62]

The JCT's scoring conventions limit the potential revenue to be earned from taxing capital gains as well as dividends at ordinary rates. For example, the static estimate for revenue from capital gains, from tax expenditure estimates, is $113 billion, but the estimate using JCT's realizations response is only $10 billion, which would allow a reduction of a percentage point.[63] If its realizations elasticity is too large, there may be a much larger gain; for example, using an elasticity recently used by the Congressional Budget Office to project realizations, revenue would be $44 billion and allow an additional reduction of 3.5 percentage points, leading to a corporate rate about 6 points lower, at 29%.[64] Another possibility is to raise rates and tax corporate stock by marking to market so individuals will be taxed on accruals whether they realize gains or not.[65] Because corporate stock is probably more responsive than other sorts of assets, and because this treatment would expand the base to include currently unrealized gains, considerable revenue might be raised.

The corporate tax rate could also be lowered by disallowing part or all of the deduction for interest. Current treatment, which allows a deduction for nominal interest, creates a negative effective tax on the investments rate.[66] Another revenue-raising approach would be to tax more pass-through firms (larger partnerships and Subchapter S firms that are corporations taxed as partnerships) at the corporate level. Also, the statutory corporate rate could be reduced by base-broadening provisions. Base broadening may lower the statutory rate but probably would not lower the effective rate that matters for investment.[67]

A lower U.S. corporate tax is desirable if one believes the most serious distortion in the international tax system is the tendency of capital to flow to low-tax foreign jurisdictions because of deferral. Lower corporate tax rates are also responsive to concerns that portfolio substitution disfavors U.S.-owned firms. Nevertheless, even notable reductions in the U.S. tax rate are unlikely to have significant effects on overall U.S. output because the corporate tax is relatively small compared with GDP. A recent estimate suggests that lowering the rate to 25% without making any other changes would increase U.S. output by only two-tenths of 1% of GDP.[68]

Although international concerns should not necessarily dominate the issues surrounding corporate tax policy,[69] they do suggest the economic desirability of certain types of corporate tax reforms that would improve economic efficiency in the international area.

End Notes

[1] Data on trade, U.S. assets abroad, and foreign assets in the United States are from the website of the U.S. Department of Commerce, Bureau of Economic Analysis, at http://www.bea. gov.

[2] International tax reform has been of interest for many years. The current tax reform drive might be dated from President Bush's executive order (E.O. 13369) establishing his advisory panel on tax reform, which cited international competitiveness concerns as one principal reason for considering tax reform. The panel's final report included a fundamental change in the structure of the U.S. international system as part of one of its reform options. See President's Advisory Panel on Federal Tax Reform, Simple, Fair, and Pro-Growth: Proposals to Fix America's Tax System, Washington, DC, November 2005. Also, beginning in 2005, Senator Ron Wyden (now chairman of the Senate Finance Committee) introduced the first of several tax reform bills that included important international elements (from the 109th Congress through the 112th, S. 1927, S. 1111, S. 3018, and S. 727). Subsequently, the President's Bipartisan Fiscal Commission (informally known as the Simpson-Bowles Commission) in February 2010 proposed a general outline of tax reform and specified international tax revisions. See National Fiscal Commission on Fiscal Responsibility and Reform, The Moment of Truth, The White House, December 2010, http://www.fiscal commission.gov/sites/fiscalcommission.gov/files/documents/TheMomentofTruth12_1_201 0.pdf. Most recently, the 2014 proposal by Ways and Means Committee Chairman Dave Camp, the Tax Reform Act of 2014 (H.R. 1), included a major change in the international corporate tax system.

[3] Of the 34 member nations of the Organization for Economic Cooperation and Development (OECD), 28 have some version of a territorial tax by treaty or statute. The territorial countries are Australia, Austria, Belgium, Canada, Czech Republic, Denmark, Estonia, Finland, France, Germany, Greece, Hungary, Iceland, Italy, Japan, Luxembourg, Netherlands, New Zealand, Norway, Poland, Portugal, Slovakia, Slovenia, Spain, Sweden, Switzerland, Turkey, and the United Kingdom. Many countries that have some version of a territorial tax restrict their exemption of foreign-source income in some way. For example, Poland and Greece apply territorial treatment only to subsidiaries in the European Union. The following countries taxed foreign-source income and rely on foreign tax credits to relieve double taxation: Chile, Ireland, Israel, Korea, Mexico, and the United States. Many countries that have some version of a territorial tax restrict their exemption of foreign-source income in some way. See PriceWaterhouseCoopers, Evolution of Territorial Tax Systems in the OECD, at http://www.techceocouncil.org/clientuploads/reports/ Report%20on%20Territorial%20Tax%20Systems_20130402b.pdf. In a list of the territorial and worldwide tax systems of the 50 largest economies, 20 had worldwide systems, 26 had territorial systems, and 4 were unspecified. Of large countries outside the OECD, China, Brazil, and India had worldwide systems and Russia had a territorial system. This source lists Poland as a worldwide system and Israel as a territorial one. See Ernst and Young,

Corporate Income tax (CIT) rates Corporate Income Tax (CIT) Rates: Largest 50 "Economies" or "Jurisdictions" by GDP, Sorted by Tax Rate, http://www.ey.com/GL/en/Services/Tax/Tax-policy-and-controversy/TPC-Briefing—Corporate-income-tax—CIT—rates.

[4] According to Internal Revenue Service (IRS) data for 2010, before-tax earnings and profits of foreign subsidiaries were $818 billion whereas branch gross income was $150 billion. The data are posted on the IRS website at http://www.irs.gov/uac/SOI-Tax-Stats-Corporate-Foreign-Tax-Credit-Statistics.

[5] U.S. parent firms are permitted to claim foreign tax credits for foreign taxes paid by their foreign-chartered subsidiaries. Such indirect credits can be claimed by the parent when the foreign-source income is remitted as dividends.

[6] Jennifer Gravelle reports 62% of income in 2008 was earned by firms with excess credits in at least one basket. See "Who Will Benefit from a Territorial Tax: Characteristics of Multinational Firms," NTA Proceedings from the 105th Annual Conference in Providence, RI, 2012, http://www.ntanet.org/images/stories/pdf/proceedings/12/15_gravelle.pdf. Similar shares were found in the past. See Rosanne Altshuler and Harry Grubert, 'Corporate Taxes in the World Economy: Reforming the Taxation of Cross-Border Income," in Fundamental Tax Reform: Issues, Choices and Implications, Ed. John W. Diamond and George R. Zodrow (Cambridge, MA: The MIT Press, 2008).

[7] For a more detailed discussion of this concept see CRS Report RS22445, Taxes and International Competitiveness, by Donald J. Marples. See also Jane G. Gravelle, "Does the Concept of Competitiveness Have Meaning in Formulating Corporate Tax Policy?" Tax Law Review, vol. 65, no. 3, 2012, p. 323-348.

[8] Comparative advantage is not a technical or unfamiliar concept; it is a common, everyday occurrence. A lawyer may be able to do his or her paralegal employee's work more efficiently, but that activity is not the best use of his or her time. A lawyer has an absolute advantage in both law practice and paralegal work but a comparative advantage in practicing law.

[9] Mihir Desai and James Hines, Evaluating International Tax Reform, National Tax Journal, vol. 56, September 2003.

[10] Michael P. Devereux, "Capital Export Neutrality, Capital Import Neutrality, Capital Ownership Neutrality, and All That," Unpublished Paper, June 11, 1990.

[11] Daniel J. Frisch, "The Economics of International Tax Policy: Some Old and New Approaches," Tax Notes, April 30, 1990.

[12] Frisch, in "The Economics of International Tax Policy: Some Old and New Approaches," states, "In short, a major element of the CIN view would seem to possess a grain of truth," (p. 590) referring to the capital import neutrality framework. Devereux, in "Capital Export Neutrality, Capital Import Neutrality, Capital Ownership Neutrality, and All That," indicated that he originally attempted to redefine capital import neutrality to cover the capital ownership neutrality concept.

[13] The concepts were first developed by Peggy Musgrave. See, for example, her United States Taxation of Foreign Investment Income: Issues and Arguments (Cambridge MA: Harvard Law School, 1969), pp. 108-121.

[14] Calculated by reducing U.S. corporate equity issues by foreign stock holdings in the United States determining U.S. holdings of foreign stocks as a share. Data on corporate equities can be found in the Board of Governors of the Federal Reserve Flow of Funds Accounts, Table L213, which can be found at http://www.federalreserve.gov/releases/Z1/ Current/. Historical series can also be found in the National Income and Product Accounts at

http://www.bea.gov/national/nipaweb/Ni_FedBeaSna/TableView.asp?SelectedTable=5&FirstYear=1998&LastYear=2005&Freq=Year.

[15] This optimality issue has also been addressed with the notion of National Ownership Neutrality, which indicates that it is both efficient and optimal to have source-based taxation.

[16] Congressional Budget Office, Corporate Tax Rates: International Comparisons, November, 2005.

[17] Data are from tax rates cited in Congressional Budget Office. Corporate Tax Rates: International Comparisons, Washington, DC, November 2005, http://www.cbo.gov/publication/17501, and portfolio share data are from U.S, Department of Treasury, Report on U.S. Portfolio Holdings of Foreign Securities, Washington, DC, 2013. http://www.treasury.gov/ticdata/Publish/shc2013_report.pdf.

[18] U.S. Department of Treasury, Report on U.S. Portfolio Holdings of Foreign Securities.

[19] Principal-agent costs occur when the objectives of the two parties are not identical. For example, the contract manufacturer (the agent) may want to increase the scale of the operation rather than maximizing profits for the firm authorizing the manufacturing (the principal).

[20] Some theories suggest that firms do not change their retentions in the steady state and the current buildup of earnings abroad is due to the possibility of a tax holiday, similar to the provision adopted in 2004 to allow a one-time exclusion of 85% of additional repatriations (payment of dividends to the parent). See CRS Report R42624, Moving to a Territorial Income Tax: Options and Challenges, by Jane G. Gravelle for a discussion of the issues surrounding the effect of taxes on repatriations.

[21] See CRS Report R42624, Moving to a Territorial Income Tax: Options and Challenges, by Jane G. Gravelle for a more extensive discussion of a territorial tax and a comparison of the details of various territorial tax proposals.

[22] Harry Grubert and John Mutti, Taxing International Business Income: Dividend Exemption versus the Current System (Washington: American Enterprise Institute, 2001), 67 pp; President's Advisory Panel on Tax Reform, Simple, Fair, and Pro-Growth: Proposals to Fix America's Tax System (Washington, 1985), pp. 239-244.

[23] National Commission on Fiscal Responsibility and Reform, The Moment of Truth, Washington, DC, The White House, December 2010.

[24] The Grubert Mutti proposal as well as proposals in a Ways and Means Committee discussion draft and the bill Senator Enzi introduced in the 112th Congress are described in CRS Report R42624, Moving to a Territorial Income Tax: Options and Challenges, by Jane G. Gravelle.

[25] Harry Grubert and John Mutti, Taxing International Business Income, p. 11. Note, however, that cross-crediting also reduces current law's inefficient disincentive to invest in high-tax countries on the part of firms without excess credits, a feature not considered by the Grubert/Mutti analysis. Because income earned by firms with a deficit of credits outweighs that of firms with excess credits, it is plausible that an exemption system's loss of this easing of inefficiency would outweigh the gains from reduced investment in low-tax countries.

[26] Writing more recently, Grubert and his co-author Rosanne Altshuler note that if an exemption system is actively considered by policy makers, its adoption with its full panoply of deduction restrictions intact would be problematic. Rosanne Altshuler and Harry Grubert, Corporate Taxes in the World Economy: Reforming the Taxation of Cross-Border Income,

unpublished paper presented at the James A. Baker II Inst. for Public Policy conference on tax reform, April 27-28, 2006, p. 4.

[27] Harry Grubert and John Mutti, Taxing International Business Income, p. 38.

[28] U.S. Congressional Budget Office, Reducing the Deficit: Spending and Revenue Option, Washington, D.C. March, 2011, p. 187, http://www.cbo.gov/sites/default/files/03-10-reducingthedeficit.pdf.

[29] Joint Committee on Taxation (JCT), Estimates of Federal Tax Expenditures 2006-2010, 99th Congress, April 25, 2006,JCS-2-06 2006 and Estimates Of Federal Tax Expenditures For Fiscal Years 2014-2018, 113th Congress, August 5, 2014, JCX-97-14. Tax expenditure documents are at https://www.jct.gov/publications.html?func=select&id=5.

[30] Edward D. Kleinbard, "Throw Territorial Taxation from the Train," Tax Notes, February 5, 2007, pp. 552-553.

[31] This proposal is described in detail in JCT, Technical Explanation of the Tax Reform Act of 2014, A Discussion Draft of the Chairman of the House Committee on Ways and Means to Reform the Internal Revenue Cost: title IV – Participation Exemption System for the Taxation of Foreign Income, JCX-15-14, February 26, 2014, https://www.jct.gov/publications.html?func=startdown&id=4557.

[32] See CRS Report R42624, Moving to a Territorial Income Tax: Options and Challenges, by Jane G. Gravelle for a more extensive discussion.

[33] The international provisions in Chairman Camp's draft proposal gained $68 billion in the FY2014-FY2023 if the transition revenues are considered but lost $102 billion, or around $10 billion a year, without them. See JCT, Estimating Revenue Effects of the Tax Reform Act of 2014, JXX-20-14, February 16, 2014, https://www.jct.gov/ publications.html?func=startdown&id=4562. Note that this estimate reflected the assumption of a 25% corporate tax rate and would have been larger if estimated in isolation. The Enzi proposal would probably have lost more revenue because it does not have an allocation of deductions.

[34] For a discussion of international tax avoidance, see CRS Report R40623, Tax Havens: International Tax Avoidance and Evasion, by Jane G. Gravelle. For a more detailed discussion of territorial tax proposals, see CRS Report R42624, Moving to a Territorial Income Tax: Options and Challenges, by Jane G. Gravelle.

[35] From 1954 to 1961, taxpayers were required to use a per-country limitation. For a synopsis of changes in limitation policy, see Thomas Horst, "The Overall vs. the Per-Country Limitation on the U.S. Foreign Tax Credit," in U.S. Department of the Treasury, Office of Tax Analysis, 1978 Compendium of Tax Research (Washington: GPO, 1978), pp. 213-214.

[36] The purest form of a separate limitation would require a separate limitation to be calculated for each investment a firm makes. Clearly, however, such a policy would present considerable administrative difficulties.

[37] Rosanne Altshuler and Harry Grubert, Corporate Taxes in the World Economy: Reforming the Taxation of Cross-Border Income, p. 17.

[38] Senate Finance Committee, Baucus Unveils Proposals for International Tax Reform, November 19, 2013, at http://www.finance.senate.gov/newsroom/chairman/release/?id=f946a9f3-d296-42ad-bae4-bcf451b34b14.

[39] The President's Framework for Business Tax Reform: A Joint Report by the White House and the Department of the Treasury, February 2012, http://www.treasury.gov/resource-center/tax-policy/Documents/The-Presidents-Frameworkfor-Business-Tax-Reform-02-22-2012.pdf.

[40] U.S. Department of Treasury, General Explanations of the Administration's Fiscal Year 2016 Revenue Proposals (Green Book), Washington, DC, February 2015, http://www.treasury.gov/resource-center/tax-policy/Documents/ General-Explanations-FY2016.pdf.

[41] The provisions of H.R. 3970 are discussed in CRS Report RL34249, The Tax Reduction and Reform Act of 2007: An Overview, by Jane G. Gravelle. The bill also contains a provision that repeals a planned liberalization of interest allocation rules for purposes of the foreign tax credit limit. This provision is discussed in CRS Report RL34494, The Foreign Tax Credit's Interest Allocation Rules, by Jane G. Gravelle and Donald J. Marples.

[42] U.S. Department of Treasury, General Explanations of the Administration's Fiscal Year 2015 Revenue Proposals (Green Book), Washington, DC, March 2014, http://www.treasury.gov/resource-center/tax-policy/Documents/GeneralExplanations-FY2015-Tables.pdf. Links to all green books can be found http://www.treasury.gov/resource-center/taxpolicy/Pages/general_explanation.aspx.

[43] U.S. Department of Treasury, General Explanations of the Administration's Fiscal Year 2010 Revenue Proposals (Green Book), Washington, DC, May 2009, http://www.treasury.gov/resource-center/tax-policy/Documents/GeneralExplanations-FY2010.pdf.

[44] Reducing taxable income in a U.S. subsidiary of a foreign firm or shifting income in general out of high-tax countries is referred to as earnings stripping.

[45] See CRS Report R43568, Corporate Expatriation, Inversions, and Mergers: Tax Issues, by Donald J. Marples and Jane G. Gravelle for a further discussion of inversions.

[46] See CRS Report R40623, Tax Havens: International Tax Avoidance and Evasion, by Jane G. Gravelle, for a summary of enacted revisions.

[47] The President's Framework for Business Tax Reform: A Joint Report by the White House and the Department of the Treasury, February 2012, http://www.treasury.gov/resource-center/tax-policy/Documents/The-Presidents-Frameworkfor-Business-Tax-Reform-02-22-2012.pdf.

[48] CRS Report R40623, Tax Havens: International Tax Avoidance and Evasion, by Jane G. Gravelle.

[49] Ibid., see Table 4.See also CRS Report R44013, Corporate Tax Base Erosion and Profit Shifting (BEPS): An Examination of the Data, by Mark P. Keightley and Jeffrey M. Stupak, for an examination of investment flows.

[50] See CRS Report R43568, Corporate Expatriation, Inversions, and Mergers: Tax Issues, by Donald J. Marples and Jane G. Gravelle.

[51] For a discussion of tax havens and illegal activities, see Martin A. Sullivan, "Sex, Drugs, and Tax Evasion," Tax Notes, June 18, 2007, pp. 1098-1100.

[52] 2002 IRS data on U.S.-controlled foreign subsidiaries show that subsidiaries pay, on average, a lower percentage of their pretax earnings in tax than do firms in the United States. This is true even for developed countries such as the United Kingdom and Canada.

[53] That tax havens actually stimulate investment in nearby higher-tax countries is argued in Mihir A. Desai, C. Fritz Foley, and James R. Hines, Jr., "Do Tax Havens Divert Economic Activity?" Economics Letters, vol. 90, 2006, pp. 219-224.

[54] Senate Finance Committee Chairman Max Baucus, for example, has observed that when tax havens are used for tax evasion "the honest American taxpayers who work hard, and do not have the ability to engage in offshore activity, are left holding the bill." Sen. Max Baucus, Hearing Statement Regarding Offshore Tax Evasion, May 3, 2007, available as a Finance Committee news release at http://www.finance.senate.gov/imo/media/doc/050307mb.pdf.

[55] To illustrate, imagine a situation in which country A has exchange of information agreements both with country B and tax haven H. Country B, however, has no exchange agreement with

the tax haven. Conceivably, would-be taxpayers from country A could channel tax-saving tax-haven transactions through country B.

[56] Jeffrey Owens, Director, OECD Centre for Tax Policy and Administration, "OECD's Work in Counteracting the Use of Tax Havens to Evade Taxes," unpublished paper presented at the American Enterprise Institute, December 11, 2006. Some U.S. critics of the OECD criticized what they saw as the initiative's underlying premise that low taxes are suspect. It was indeed partly on this basis that the Bush administration persuaded the OECD to focus on transparency and exchange of information rather than efforts to persuade targeted countries to change their tax practices toward nonresidents. See Hon. Paul O'Neill, Secretary of the Treasury, testimony before the Senate Committee on Governmental Affairs, Permanent Subcommittee on Investigations, July 18, 2001, available at the committee's website, at http://hsgac.senate.gov/071801_psioneil.htm.

[57] The OECD's action plan was released in 2013. See Action Plan on Base Erosion and Profit Shifting, at http://www.oecd.org/ctp/BEPSActionPlan.pdf. Some specific proposals have been released subsequently.

[58] For a description of the proposal, see U.S. Congress, JCT, Description of Revenue Proposals Contained in the President's Fiscal Year 2001 Budget Proposals (Washington: GPO, 2000), pp. 500-509.

[59] See CRS Report R40623, Tax Havens: International Tax Avoidance and Evasion, by Jane G. Gravelle for descriptions.

[60] JCT, Estimated Revenue Effects Of The Revenue Provisions Contained In An Amendment In The Nature Of A Substitute To H.R. 8, The "American Taxpayer Relief Act Of 2012," 113th Congress, January 1, 2013, JCX-1-13, at https://www.jct.gov/publications.html?func=select&id=72.

[61] Congressional Budget Office, The Budget and Economic Outlook: 2014-2024, Washington DC, February 2014, http://www.cbo.gov/sites/default/files/45010-Outlook2014_Feb_0.pdf.

[62] See CRS Report R41364, Capital Gains Tax Options: Behavioral Responses and Revenues, by Jane G. Gravelle for formulas to make adjustments in realizations. For example, in measuring the revenue loss from keeping part of capital gains taxes at 15% rather than 20%, the estimate assumes larger realizations compared to the baseline, where a 20% rate applies.

[63] The $113 billion is the difference between the projected tax expenditure for lower rates on capital gains and dividends in the JCT's tax expenditure estimates (Estimates Of Federal Tax Expenditures For Fiscal Years 2014-2018, 113th Congress, Washington, DC, August 5, 2014, JCX-97-14) and the $22 billion estimate for the cost of taxing dividends below ordinary rates. The tax rate is assumed to rise from 20% to 37% based on the JCT's static estimate and its implied rate change as compared to the Congressional Budget Office's baseline realizations and revenues in its spreadsheet, found at http://www.cbo.gov/publication/45065.

[64] There is some evidence that suggests the JCT's response is too large as discussed in CRS Report R41364, Capital Gains Tax Options: Behavioral Responses and Revenues, by Jane G. Gravelle. This document also reports on the Congressional Budget Office adjustment.

[65] See Alan D. Viard, "Moving Away From the Realization Principle," Tax Notes, November 17, 2014, pp.847-854.

[66] See CRS Report R43432, Bonus Depreciation: Economic and Budgetary Issues, by Jane G. Gravelle for calculations.

[67] See CRS Report RL34229, Corporate Tax Reform: Issues for Congress, by Jane G. Gravelle for a more extensive discussion and estimates of how much the statutory tax rate could be reduced. Also see CRS Report R42451, Taxing Large Pass-Throughs As Corporations:

How Many Firms Would Be Affected?, by Mark P. Keightley for a discussion of how many firms and how much profit might be affected.

[68] CRS Report R41743, International Corporate Tax Rate Comparisons and Policy Implications, by Jane G. Gravelle.

[69] Two reasons to provide relief at the individual level are (1) to focus tax cuts on marginal investment, which is more likely to be taxable investment to individuals rather than investment in pension funds and retirement accounts; and (2) to reduce the distortion that capital gains taxes impose on the willingness to realize gains and adjust assets. This latter distortion, however, would be improved if an accrual basis capital gains tax on corporate stock were adopted. Such a move would also raise a great deal of revenue that could be used to lower corporate tax rates. In addition, doing so would end concerns about using corporations with lower tax rates to shelter income.

INDEX

D

E

F

G

H

I

Q

R

S